MW01206414

Dear fellow Californian,

Whether traveling by car, transit, bike, scooter, skateboard or on foot, we all want to reach our destination safely. Tragically, many Californians do not.

Since 2010, more than 30,000 people have been killed and another 100,000 people seriously injured on California roads. This deadly trend is getting worse, especially for people walking or biking. We've seen a nearly 50 percent rise in annual deaths and serious injuries for pedestrians and greater than 60 percent increase in bicyclists killed per year since 2010.

Unlike those of us traveling in vehicles with seat belts, airbags and other safety features, people outside of vehicles don't have the same level of protection and are more vulnerable every time they are on the road. Their safety must always be top of mind when we're driving.

California is doing everything possible to implement comprehensive traffic safety measures to eliminate deaths and serious injuries on our roadways. It includes strategies to reduce our dependence on driving, to the way we design roads and intersections, to expanding safe walking and biking options.

But we need your help. Without all of us practicing safe driving habits, these avoidable tragedies will continue to occur. Please make sure to buckle up, follow all traffic laws, pay extra attention to pedestrians and bicyclists, and do not drive if you're distracted or impaired.

I hope the information in this California Driver's Handbook can help everyone on the road – drivers, bicyclists and pedestrians – reach their destination safely. Because it's about more than just learning the rules of the roads. It could be a matter of life and death.

Wishing you safe journeys,

Toks Omishakin
Secretary
California State Transportation Agency

TABLE OF CONTENTS

DMV SERVICES

Have your driver's license or identification (ID) card number, vehicle license plate number, or vehicle identification number (VIN) available.

Online Services

Vehicle Registration Renewal at **dmv.ca.gov/vrservices**.

Driver's License Renewal at **dmv.ca.gov/dlservices**.

Office Appointments at **dmv.ca.gov/make-an-appointment**.

Visit **dmv.ca.gov/online** to find many other online services.

Kiosk Services

Visit **dmv.ca.gov/kiosks** to find kiosk services and locations.

Phone Services

Call 1-800-777-0133:

During normal business hours:

- Talk to a DMV representative.

Automated 24/7 Phone Services:

- Renew your vehicle registration.
- Make a DMV office appointment.

Individuals who are deaf, hard of hearing, or speech impaired may call 1-800-368-4327 for assistance.

SECTION 1. *The California Driver's License*

A California driver's license allows you to drive on public roads.

Before you can get a driver's license in California, you are required to pass the knowledge and behind-the-wheel drive tests based on information in this handbook.

You must have the correct license to drive your vehicle type. Most people need a noncommercial Class C driver's license. To operate commercial vehicles, motorcycles, and other types of vehicles, you must have a different class of license.

For information on vehicles covered by a Class C, visit **dmv.ca.gov/dl**.

CARD DESIGNATIONS

REAL ID Driver's License
Beginning May 2025, your driver's license or identification (ID) card must be REAL ID compliant if you use it to:

- Board an airplane for domestic flights.
- Enter military bases.
- Enter most federal facilities.

Visit **dmv.ca.gov/realid** to learn more about applying for a REAL ID.

Driver's Licenses for Undocumented Residents
California offers driver's licenses for all residents regardless of immigration status. For more information, visit **dmv.ca.gov/dl**.

Organ and Tissue Donor
For information, visit **donateLIFEcalifornia.org**.

Veterans
Visit **dmv.ca.gov/veterans** to learn more about the requirements and benefits of a Veteran designation.

ID Cards
ID cards are issued for identification purposes to eligible persons of any age. They do not permit you to drive. To get an ID, you must provide your identity document, residency documents, and social security number.

Visit **dmv.ca.gov/id-cards** to complete an ID card application and get information on current acceptable documents and reduced-fee, no-fee, or senior ID cards.

BUCKLE UP
EVERY TIME

Do it for **YOU**
and those **YOU LOVE**

SECTION 2. *Getting an Instruction Permit and Driver's License*

If you do not have a driver's license from California or another state, you must apply for an instruction permit before taking the behind-the-wheel drive test to get your driver's license.

WHAT YOU NEED

To apply for an instruction permit or driver's license, you must provide:

- **Proof of identity:** Proving who you are.
- **Two proofs of residency:** Proving you live in California. Exceptions may apply.
- **Legal full name document:** Proving your current name if the name on your identity document and application do not match.
- **Social security number:** Exceptions may apply.

For REAL ID requirements, current acceptable documents, and eligibility, visit **dmv.ca.gov/realid**.

REGISTER TO VOTE

For information on registering to vote, visit California Secretary of State at **sos.ca.gov**.

APPLYING FOR AN INSTRUCTION PERMIT

To apply for a Class C instruction permit:

1. Complete a Driver's License & ID Card Application.
2. Provide your documents.
3. Pay a non-refundable application fee.
4. Pass your knowledge test(s).
5. Pass a vision test.

For more information, visit **dmv.ca.gov/instructionpermit** for a complete list of application steps and requirements.

If you are under 18 years old, you will also need to:

- Be at least 15½ years old.
- Complete a driver education program.
- Have a parent or guardian sign to approve the application and accept financial responsibility (see Section 10). If your parents or guardians share joint custody of you, both must sign.
- Wait to use your instruction permit until you start behind-the-wheel driver training with an instructor who will validate the permit.

DRIVING SCHOOLS

Driver education and driver training are offered at DMV-licensed driving schools and some high schools. Instructors must carry an instructor's ID card. Ask to see it.

See the Driver Training Schools page at **dmv.ca.gov/driver-ed** for more information about selecting a driving school.

APPLYING FOR A DRIVER'S LICENSE

To get your driver's license after you have your instruction permit, you need to:

- Practice driving with a California-licensed driver who is at least 18 years old (25 for minors). This person must sit close enough to take control of the vehicle if needed.
- Pass a behind-the-wheel drive test.

If you are under 18 years old, you will also need to:

- Be at least 16 years old.
- Have an instruction permit from California or another state for at least 6 months (or turn 18 years old) before scheduling your behind-the-wheel drive test.
- Prove that you completed **both** driver education and driver training.
- Practice driving for at least 50 hours with a California-licensed driver who is at least 25 years old. Ten hours must be at night.

See the Driver's Licenses page at **dmv.ca.gov/dlservices** for the complete list of application steps, requirements, the Parent Teen Driving Contract, and Driving Performance Evaluation (DPE) Score Sheet.

Minor's Restrictions and Exceptions

When you are under 18 years old, your driver's license will have the word provisional. As a provisional driver, you **cannot** drive:

- Between 11 p.m. and 5 a.m. during the first 12 months you have your license.
- With passengers under 20 years old, unless your parent or guardian or other California-licensed driver (at least 25 years old) rides with you.
- For pay or operate vehicles that require a commercial Class A, B, or C license.

There are exceptions to these restrictions if you:

- Have a medical need and cannot reasonably find another way to travel. You must carry a note signed by your physician. The note must have your medical condition and date you are expected to recover.
- Drive for schooling or a school activity. You must carry a note signed by your school principal, dean, or designee.
- Must drive for work reasons. You must carry a note signed by your employer. The note must confirm your employment.
- Must drive an immediate family member. You must carry a note signed by your parent or legal guardian. The note must state the reason you need to drive, the family member, and date when the need will end.

NOTE: A parent or guardian may cancel their teen's license by completing a Request for Cancellation or Surrender of a Driver License or ID Card form.

SECTION 3. *The Testing Process*

DRIVER'S LICENSE TESTS

Here is an overview of the driver's license tests:

1. Vision Test

DMV tests all applicants to ensure they can see well enough to drive safely. If you take your vision test with corrective or contact lenses, your driver's license will have a corrective lenses restriction. If you do not pass your vision test, you will be asked to have your eye doctor complete a Report of Vision Examination form. For more information, visit **dmv.ca.gov/vision-standards**.

2. Knowledge Test

When you apply for an original driver's license, you must pass a knowledge test with multiple choice questions. You are allowed three attempts to pass before you must reapply. Minors must wait seven days to retake a failed knowledge test, not including the day of the failure.

Testing options will be available once you complete your application at **dmv.ca.gov/dl**.

IMPORTANT: You are not allowed to use any testing aids during knowledge tests, such as a California Driver's Handbook or cell phone.

3. Behind-the-Wheel Drive Test

When you apply for an original driver's license, you will be tested on your ability to safely drive a vehicle. Upon renewal, drivers with a vision or medical condition may be required to take a behind-the-wheel test. The examiner may give two or more instructions at one time to determine whether you can understand and properly follow both directions. For example, "At the next street, make a left turn, and then at the first intersection make another left turn."

Visit **dmv.ca.gov/make-an-appointment** to schedule a behind-the-wheel drive test appointment.

On the day of your behind-the-wheel test, you must bring:

1. Your instruction permit or driver's license (if you have one).
2. Another California-licensed driver who is at least 18 years old (25 for minors), unless you are already licensed to drive.
3. A vehicle that is safe to drive for your test.
4. Valid proof of insurance and vehicle registration.
5. If you plan to use a rental vehicle for your drive test, your name must be listed on the rental contract. The contract must not exclude behind-the-wheel drive tests.

NOTE: Minors must wait 14 days to retake a failed behind-the-wheel drive test, not including the day of the failure.

Before you begin, the DMV examiner will ask you to locate and demonstrate the following:

- **Driver window** – The window on the driver side must open.
- **Windshield** – The windshield must allow a full, clear, unblocked view for you and the DMV examiner. Windshield cracks may postpone your test.
- **Rear-view mirrors** – At least two rearview mirrors. One of them must be on the left side of your vehicle.
- **Brake lights** – The right and left brake lights must be operational.
- **Tires** – The tires must have at least 1/32-inch of uniformed tread depth. The use of a donut tire is not allowed during a drive test.
- **Foot brake** – There must be at least one inch of clearance between the bottom of the brake pedal and the floorboard when depressed.
- **Horn** – Designed for the vehicle, in proper working condition, and loud enough to be heard from a distance of at least 200 feet.
- **Emergency (parking brake)** – How to set and release the parking brake.
- **Turn/Arm signals**
  a. Left turn.
  b. Right turn.
  c. Slowing down or stopping.
- **Windshield wipers: control arm or switch** – You may be required to show they function.
- **Seat belts** – All seat belts must work properly and be used by the individual(s) in the vehicle.

NOTE: If your vehicle does not meet the requirements, your drive test will be rescheduled.

Interpreters may be used during the pre-drive inspection for the identification and use of certain controls in the vehicle but may not accompany you during the drive test.

Only the examiner is allowed to accompany you during the drive test. Exceptions are made for training, service animals, and certain law enforcement situations.

The use of a recording device, including a video recorder, is prohibited during a behind-the-wheel drive test. If the recording device cannot be powered off or disabled, the applicant must block it so there is no visual or audio recording during the drive test.

Other Things to Know for Your Behind-the-Wheel Test

The drive test is intended to determine your skill in operating a motor vehicle in most road situations and evaluate your abilities, not the vehicle's technology. Therefore, advanced driver assistance systems technologies, such as automated parallel parking, lane departure, and adaptive cruise control, are not permitted during the drive test. Vehicle safety technology, such as backup cameras and blind spot monitors, may be used on the drive test, but are not a replacement for an actual visual check of your mirrors and blind spots.

To view a sample of the Driving Performance Evaluation (DPE) Score Sheet, visit **dmv.ca.gov/teendriver**. For a sample of the Supplemental/Area DPE Score Sheet, visit **dmv.ca.gov/seniors**.

SECTION 4. *Changing, Replacing, and Renewing Your Driver's License*

Changes to Your License

If you legally change your name or need an update to your driver's license, such as your physical description or gender identity, visit **dmv.ca.gov/dlservices**.

Change Your Address

If you move, you must notify DMV of your new address within ten days. Submit a change of address online at **dmv.ca.gov/addresschange** or by mail. It is your responsibility to ensure DMV has your correct mailing address on record.

You do not automatically get a new driver's license when you change your address. You may request a replacement for a fee.

Replace or Renew Your Driver's License

It is against the law to drive with an expired driver's license. To renew or replace a lost, stolen, or damaged driver's license, visit **dmv.ca.gov/dlservices**, or DMV office.

Before DMV can issue you a driver's license, you may need to provide additional proof of your identity. Your driver's license and identity document may expire on the same date. If so, you will be required to provide a valid identity document. If you are a minor, your parent or guardian must sign the application. Once you receive your replacement card, your old card is no longer valid. If you find the old card, destroy it.

Extend Your Driver's License

If you are out-of-state and cannot renew, you may request a one year extension of your driver's license. Before your driver's license expires, submit a request with your name, driver's license number, birth date, California residence address, and out-of-state address to **dl-extensions@dmv.ca.gov**.

NOTE: Limited-term driver's licenses are not eligible for this extension.

DMV KIOSKS
Offer Convenient Transactions

Available at:
    Grocery Stores
    DMV Offices
    Auto Clubs

STATE OF CALIFORNIA
DMV
Department of Motor Vehicles

Find a kiosk near you
dmv.ca.gov/kiosks

✓ Complete your vehicle registration renewal

✓ Receive a replacement registration card or sticker

✓ Submit proof of insurance

✓ File for planned nonoperation (PNO) status

✓ Obtain your driver's record and vehicle record

✓ Receive a replacement driver's license and more . . .

SECTION 5. *An Introduction to Driving*

Your health may affect your driving.

Vision – You must be able to notice hazards in different types of lighting, judge distances, adjust to traffic speed, and read road signs.

Hearing – You must be able to hear horns, sirens, motorcycles, or screeching tires that may alert you of hazards. It is illegal to wear a headset or earplugs in both ears while driving.

Fatigue and Drowsiness – Can affect your vision and increase reaction time to hazards.

Physical and Mental – You must be alert to quickly decide the correct course of action in any type of traffic situation, including unexpected ones.

Medications – Prescription and over-the-counter medications can make you an unsafe driver. Some medicines can make you sleepy. It is your responsibility to know the effects of the medications you take.

Health – Physicians are required to report patients, who are at least 14 years old, to DMV if they believe you have medical conditions that may affect your ability to drive safely, such as lapse of consciousness.

Controlling the Vehicle

To control your vehicle, it is critical to keep both hands on the wheel whenever possible.

Hand-to-Hand Steering

To use this steering wheel method:

1. Start with your hands at 9 and 3 o'clock or 8 and 4 o'clock.
2. Do not cross your hands over the middle of the steering wheel.
3. Keep your hands in these positions, even when making turns.

Hand-Over-Hand Steering

Use this steering wheel method when you turn at low speeds, park, or need to recover from a skid. To use this method:

1. Start with your hands at 8 and 4 o'clock.
2. Reach across the steering wheel to grasp the opposite side.
3. Let go of the steering wheel with your other hand.
4. Reach across the arm still holding the wheel, grip the wheel, and pull up.

One-Hand Steering

There are only two situations that may require steering with one hand:

- When you are turning while backing up to see where you are going behind you. Place your hand at the 12 o'clock position on the steering wheel.
- When you are operating vehicle controls that require you to remove a hand from the steering wheel.

SIGNALS, HORNS, AND HEADLIGHTS

Your signals, horn, and headlights are important for communicating with other drivers, pedestrians, and bicyclists.

Signaling

Always signal when you turn, change lanes, slow down, or stop.

You can signal using your vehicle's signal lights or using hand-and-arm positions. Bicyclists may signal a turn with their arm held straight out, pointing in the direction they plan to turn.

Left Turn	Right Turn	Slow or Stop

You should signal:

- At least 100 feet before you turn.
- Before every lane change.
- At least five seconds before you change lanes on a freeway.
- Before pulling next to the curb or away from the curb.
- Even when you do not see other vehicles around you.
- When you are almost through the intersection if you plan to turn shortly after crossing the intersection.

Remember to turn off your signal when you no longer need it.

Using Your Horn

Use your vehicle's horn to let other drivers know you are there or warn others of a hazard. Use your horn to:

- Avoid collisions.
- Alert oncoming traffic on narrow mountain roads where you cannot see at least 200 feet ahead.

Using Your Headlights

Your vehicle's headlights help you see what is in front of you. They also make it easier for other drivers to see your vehicle. Dim your high-beam headlights to low beams within 500 feet of a vehicle coming toward you or within 300 feet of a vehicle you are following. It is illegal to drive using only parking lights. Use your headlights:

- When it is too dark to see from 1,000 feet away.
- Beginning 30 minutes after sunset.
- Until 30 minutes before sunrise.
- In adverse weather. If you need to use your windshield wipers due to fog, rain, or snow, you must turn on your low-beam headlights.
- When conditions (such as clouds, dust, smoke, or fog) prevent you from seeing other vehicles.
- On mountain roads and tunnels (even on sunny days).
- When a road sign states that headlights must be on.
- To help other drivers see your vehicle, especially when the sun is low on the horizon.

Using Your Emergency Flashers

If you can see a collision or hazard ahead, warn drivers behind you using these methods:

- Turn on your emergency flashers.
- Lightly tap your brake pedal three or four times.
- Use a hand signal when slowing and stopping.

If you need to stop because of vehicle trouble:

- Turn on your emergency flashers. If your vehicle does not have emergency flashers, use your turn signals.
- If possible, pull off the road away from all traffic.
- If you cannot get completely off the road, stop where people can see you and your vehicle from behind.
- Do not stop just over a hill or just around a curve. Other drivers may not see your vehicle in time to avoid a collision.
- Call for emergency roadside assistance and stay in your vehicle until help arrives.

SECTION 6. *Navigating the Roads*

TRAFFIC LANES
A traffic lane is a section of road for a single line of traffic.

Lane Markings
Lane markings on road surfaces help drivers know which part of the road to use and understand traffic rules.

Single Solid Yellow Line
A single solid yellow line marks the center of a road with two-way traffic. Do not pass a vehicle in front of you if there is only one lane of traffic going your direction and a solid yellow line on your side of the road.

Double Solid Yellow Lines
Do not pass over double solid yellow lines. Stay to the right of these lines unless you are:

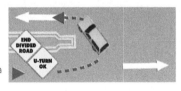

- In a high-occupancy vehicle (HOV) carpool lane that has a designated entrance on the left.
- Instructed by construction or other signs to drive on the other side of the road because your side is closed or blocked.
- Turning left across a single set of double yellow lines to enter or exit a driveway or private road or make a U-turn.

Two sets of solid double yellow lines spaced two or more feet apart are considered a barrier. Do not drive on or over this barrier, make a left turn, or make a U-turn across it, except at designated openings.

Broken Yellow Line

A broken yellow line indicates you may pass if the broken line is next to your driving lane. Only pass when it is safe.

Single Solid White Line
A single solid white line marks traffic lanes going in the same direction. This includes one-way streets.

Double Solid White Lines

Double solid white lines indicate a lane barrier between a regular use and a preferential use lane, such as a carpool (HOV) lane. You may also see double solid white lines in or near freeway on and off ramps. Never change lanes over double solid white lines. Wait until you see a single broken white line.

Broken White Lines

Broken white lines separate traffic lanes on roads with two or more lanes in the same direction.

End of Lane Markings

Ending freeway and street lanes are usually marked with large broken lines. If you are driving in a lane marked with broken lines, be prepared to exit the freeway or for the lane to end. Look for a sign that tells you to exit or merge.

Yield Line

A yield line is a solid white line of triangles that shows approaching vehicles where to yield or stop. The triangles point towards approaching vehicles.

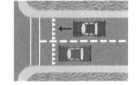

Choosing a Lane

Traffic lanes are often referred to by number. The left (or fast) lane is called the Number 1 Lane. The lane to the right of the Number 1

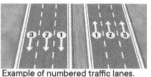

Example of numbered traffic lanes.

Lane is called the Number 2 Lane. Then the Number 3 Lane, etc.

Here are some tips for choosing a lane:

- Use the left lane to pass or turn left.
- Use the right lane to enter or exit traffic.

Changing Lanes

Before you change lanes:

- Signal.
- Check your mirrors.
- Check traffic behind and beside you.
- Look over your shoulder in the direction you plan to move to make sure the lane is clear.
- Check your blind spots for other vehicles, motorcyclists, and bicyclists. Do not let the vehicle drift into another lane.
- Be sure there is enough space for your vehicle in the next lane. It is not necessary to slow down before a lane change.

Stay in one lane as much as possible. Do not weave in and out of traffic. Last minute lane or direction changes may increase the risk of collisions. Once you start moving through an intersection, keep going. If you start to make a turn, follow through. If you miss a turn, keep driving until you can safely and legally turn around.

Types of Lanes

Passing Lanes

On a multilane road, the passing lane (far left lane) is the lane closest to the center divider and is used to pass other vehicles.

Carpool/High-Occupancy Vehicle (HOV) Lanes

An HOV lane is a special lane reserved for carpools, buses, motorcycles, or low-emission vehicles with decals. To use an HOV lane, one of these must apply:

- You have a certain number of people in your vehicle. There will be signs at the on-ramp or along the road to tell you the minimum number of people. Road signs also list the hours when the HOV rules apply.
- You are driving a low emission or zero emission vehicle. You must display a special DMV-issued decal.
- You are riding a motorcycle (unless otherwise posted).

The road surface in a HOV lane is marked with a diamond symbol and the words Carpool Lane. Do not cross over double solid lines to enter or exit an HOV lane. Use designated entrances and exits.

Center Left Turn Lanes
A center left turn lane is located in the middle of a two-way street. It is marked on both sides by two painted lines. The inner line is broken and the outer line is solid. Use the center left turn lane to prepare for and make a left turn or U-turn. It is not a regular traffic lane or passing lane. You may only drive for 200 feet in the center left turn lane. To turn left from this lane:

- Look for other vehicles coming toward you in the center left turn lane.
- Signal.
- Look over your shoulder to check your blind spots.
- Merge completely into the center left turn lane so you do not block traffic.
- Turn when it is safe.

Turnout Areas or Lanes
Some two-lane roads have special turnout areas or lanes. Merge into these areas or lanes to allow cars behind you to pass.

SLOWER
TRAFFIC
USE
TURNOUTS

You must use a turnout area or lane to let other vehicles pass when you are driving slowly on a two-lane road, where passing is unsafe, and there are five or more vehicles following you.

Bicycle Lanes

Bicycle lanes are for bicyclists only and run alongside vehicle traffic. They are typically marked by a single solid white line and signs. They are sometimes painted bright green to make them easier to see.

It is illegal to drive in a bicycle lane unless you are:

- Parking (where permitted).
- Entering or leaving the road.
- Turning (within 200 feet of an intersection).

There are multiple types of bike lanes and markings:

- **Bike lane:** Established along streets adjacent to vehicle traffic. Typically marked by a single solid white line that turns into a dash-line near an intersection.

- **Buffered bike lane:** Uses chevrons or diagonal markings to provide greater separation from traffic and on-street parking.

- **Bike route:** Uses bike route signs and shared road markings to designate a preferred route for bicyclists on streets shared with vehicle traffic.

- **Bicycle boulevard:** Prioritizes bicycle travel on streets shared with vehicle traffic.

- **Separated bikeway:** Is physically separated from motor vehicle traffic and for exclusive use of bicyclists. They are also known as a cycle track or protected bike lanes. The separation may include flexible posts, grade separation, inflexible barriers, or on-street parking.

- **Shared roadway bicycle markings:** Alert drivers that bicyclists can occupy the lane and help bicyclists maintain a safe lane position in traffic.

Example of shared roadway.

NOTE: Check your blind spots before entering a bike lane. If you drive a motorized bicycle, use caution to avoid other bicyclists. Travel at a reasonable speed and do not endanger the safety of other bicyclists.

Turns

Right Turns

To make a right turn:

- Drive close to the right edge of the road.
  - If a designated right turn lane is available, enter at the opening.
  - You can drive in a bike lane within 200 feet from the turn. Check for bicyclists in your blind spots.

Example of a right turn.

- Watch for pedestrians, bicyclists, or motorcyclists between your vehicle and the curb.
- Start signaling about 100 feet before the turn.
- Look over your right shoulder and reduce your speed.
- Stop behind the limit line. A limit line is a wide white line that shows the drivers where to stop before an intersection or crosswalk. If there is no limit line, stop before you enter the crosswalk. If there is no crosswalk, stop before you enter the intersection.
- Look both ways (left-right-left) and turn when it is safe.
- Complete your turn in the right lane. Do not turn wide into another lane.

Right Turn Against a Red Light

You may turn right at a red light after a complete stop unless there is a No Turn on Red sign. Follow the same steps listed above for right turns.

Right Turn Against a Red Arrow

You may not turn right if you are stopped at a red arrow light. Wait until the light changes to green before making your turn.

Right Turn at a Public Transit Bus Lane

It is illegal to drive, stop, park, or leave a vehicle in an area designated for public transit buses. Signs will be posted to indicate the lanes are for bus only use. However, you may cross a bus lane to make a right turn.

Right Turn onto a Road with a Dedicated Lane

A dedicated right turn lane does not merge into another lane and allows you to make a right turn without stopping. You may make your turn even if there is a red light for vehicles going straight through the intersection. If there is a traffic light or sign on the right curb of the right turn lane, you must obey that light or sign. Always yield to pedestrians in a crosswalk when turning.

Left Turns

To turn left:

- Drive close to the center divider or into the left turn lane.

Example of a left turn.

  - Enter a designated left turn lane at the opening. Do not cross any solid line.
  - Enter a two-way center left turn lane within 200 feet of the turn. Respect the right-of-way of any vehicle, bicyclist, or motorcyclist already in the lane. Always yield to pedestrians.
- Start signaling 100 feet before the turn.
- Look over your left shoulder and reduce your speed.
- Stop behind the limit line. If there is no limit line, stop before you enter the crosswalk. If there is no crosswalk, stop before you enter the intersection.
- Look both ways (left-right-left) and begin your turn when it is safe.
- Proceed into the intersection while turning to complete your turn in the left lane.
- Do not turn the steering wheel too soon and enter the lane of oncoming vehicles.

  - Keep your wheels pointed straight ahead until it is safe to start your turn. If your wheels are pointed to the left and a vehicle hits you from behind, you could be pushed into oncoming traffic.
- Accelerate smoothly during and after the turn.
- Allow the steering wheel to straighten in the new lane.

Left Turn Against a Red Light

You may turn left against a red light when you are turning from a one-way street onto a one-way street. Make sure there is no sign prohibiting the turn. Yield to other vehicles, pedestrians, or bicyclists who have a green light. Look both ways and turn when it is safe.

U-turns

A U-turn is when you turn your vehicle around to go back in the direction you came. To make a U-turn, signal and use the left turn lane or far-left lane. You may make a U-turn:

- Across a double yellow line.
- In a residential district if no vehicles are approaching you within 200 feet.
- At an intersection on a green traffic light or green arrow, unless a No U-turn sign is posted.
- On a divided highway if a center divider opening is provided.

Never make a U-turn:

- Where a No U-turn sign is posted.
- At or on a railroad crossing.
- On a divided highway by crossing a dividing section, curb, strip of land, or two sets of double yellow lines.
- When you cannot see clearly for 200 feet in each direction.
- On a one-way street.
- In front of a fire station. **Never** use a fire station driveway to turn around.
- In business districts (the part of a city or town where most offices and businesses are).

Examples of Turns

The descriptions below refer to the numbers next to the cars in the images. Watch for pedestrians, motorcycles, and bicycles between your vehicle and the curb. When making turns, there may be signs or arrows that indicate you can turn from or end in more than one lane.

1. **Left turn from a two-way street.** Start the turn in the left lane closest to the middle of the street. To reduce the risk of collision, end the turn in the left lane closest to the middle of the street going in your vehicle's direction.

2. **Right turn.** Begin and end the turn in the lane closest to the right edge of the road. Do not swing wide into another lane of traffic.

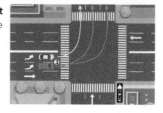

3. **Left turn from a two-way street onto a one-way street.** Start the turn from the lane closest to the middle of the street (far-left lane). If there are three or more lanes in your direction of travel, you may end your turn in any lane that is open.

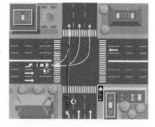

4. **Left turn from a one-way street onto a two-way street.** Start the turn from the far-left lane. To reduce the risk of collision, end the turn in the left lane closest to the middle of the street going in your vehicle's direction.

5. **Left turn from a one-way street onto a one-way street.** Start the turn from the far-left lane. Bicyclists can legally use the left turn lane for their left turns. If there are three or more lanes in your direction of travel, you may end your turn in any lane that is open.

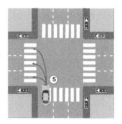

6. **Right turn from a one-way street onto a one-way street.** Start the turn in the far-right lane. If safe, you may end the turn in any lane.

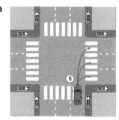

7. **Turn at a "T" intersection from a one-way street onto a two-way street.** Traffic going straight through the intersection has the right-of-way. You may turn either right or left from the center lane.

Braking

- Remove your foot from the gas pedal (accelerator) and allow the vehicle to slow down. Lightly press the brake until you come to a full stop. Give yourself enough space and time to perform this maneuver.
- When stopping at a limit line, do not cross over the line. If stopping behind a vehicle, leave enough space to see their rear wheels.

Merging and Exiting

Merging

Highway traffic has the right-of-way. For more information, see Right-of-Way Rules: Who Goes First in Section 7. When you enter a highway, you will need to:

- Be in the proper lane on the on-ramp.
- Be at or near the speed of traffic.
- Merge into highway traffic when safe to do so. Do not stop unless absolutely necessary.
- Merge into a space large enough for your vehicle to safely join the lane.
- Use your mirrors and turn signals.
- Turn your head quickly to look over your shoulder before changing lanes or merging into traffic.
- Make sure you can stop safely by leaving three seconds of space between you and the vehicle in front of you.
- Do not cross over any solid lines when merging. If you need to cross several lanes, signal and cross them one at a time. Check your blind spots for vehicles, motorcyclists, bicyclists, and pedestrians each time.

Exiting

To exit a highway safely:

- Know your exit and be aware of when it is approaching.
- If you plan to change lanes, do so one at a time. Signal and look over your shoulder to check your blind spots.
- When in the proper lane, signal five seconds (approximately 400 feet) before you exit.
- Make sure you are at a safe speed to exit.
- Do not cross over any solid lines when exiting.

Crossing or Entering Traffic

When entering traffic from a full stop, signal and leave a large enough space to get up to the speed of traffic. To merge, enter, or exit traffic, you need a space that is:

- Half a block on city streets, which is about 150 feet.
- A full block on the highway, which is about 300 feet.
- Even if you have a green light, do not start across the intersection if there are pedestrians or vehicles blocking your pathway.

When turning left, do not assume that an oncoming vehicle with its right turn signal on is turning before it reaches you. The driver may have their signal on by mistake or plan to turn just beyond you. Wait for the vehicle to start its turn before beginning the left turn.

PASSING

You must judge whether you have enough space to pass whenever you approach:

- An oncoming vehicle or bicyclist.
- A hill, curve, intersection, or road obstruction. To safely pass, the hill or curve should be at least one-third of a mile ahead.

Before you pass, look ahead for road conditions that may cause other vehicles to move into your lane.

Do not pass:

- If you are approaching a hill or curve and cannot see if other traffic is approaching. This is very dangerous on one and two lane roads.
- Within 100 feet of an intersection, bridge, tunnel, railroad crossing, or other hazardous area.
- At crossroads and driveways.
- Unless you have enough space to return to your lane.

How to Pass

When you are going to pass on an open highway:

- Signal that you plan on passing.
- Look over your shoulder to check your blind spots.
- Drive into the passing lane.
- Speed up to pass the vehicle.
- Signal and return to your original lane.

You may pass on the right only when:

- An open highway has two or more lanes going in your direction.
- The driver ahead of you is turning left and you can safely pass on the right. Never pass on the left if the driver is signaling a left turn.
- You are on a one-way street.

Never drive off the paved or main-traveled part of the road to pass.

Being Passed

If a vehicle is passing you or signals that they plan on passing, allow the vehicle to pass. Maintain your lane position and your speed.

PARKING

Parallel Parking

Parallel parking is when you park in line with the road and other parked vehicles. To parallel park:

1. **Find a space.** Look for a space at least three feet longer than your vehicle. When you find a space, turn on your signal to show that you plan on parking.

2. **Pull up alongside the vehicle in front of the space.** Leave about two feet between your vehicle and the vehicle next to you. Stop once your rear bumper is aligned with the front of your parking space. Keep your signal on.

3. **Check your blind spots.** Look in your rearview mirror and over your shoulder for approaching vehicles and pedestrians.

4. **Begin backing up.** Turn your steering wheel to back into the space at about a 45-degree angle.

5. **Straighten out.** Begin turning the steering wheel away from the curb when your rear wheel is within 18 inches of the curb. You may need to pull forward and backward to straighten out. Your vehicle should now be parallel and within 18 inches of the curb.

6. **Parking.** Turn off your vehicle and set the parking brake. Before you exit your vehicle, look carefully for passing vehicles, bicycles, and motorcycles. Exit when safe.

Straight Line Backing

To back up in a straight line:

1. **Traffic check.** Observe traffic and check appropriate blind spots.
2. **Signal.** Activate the turn signal before pulling up to the curb. Cancel the turn signal once completed.
3. **Check your blind spots.** Look in your rearview mirror and over your shoulder for approaching vehicles and pedestrians.
4. **Begin backing up.** Back in a straight line for three vehicle lengths while remaining within three feet of the curb. Stay aware of what is behind you when backing up.
5. **Control.** To maintain control of the vehicle, back at a smooth, safe speed and adjust the steering wheel when needed. Practice until you can keep the vehicle straight. Repeat steps 1 and 2 to pull away from the curb.

Parking on a Hill

When you park on a hill, your vehicle could roll due to equipment failure. Remember to set the parking brake and leave the vehicle in park, or in gear for manual transmission. To park:

- **On a sloping driveway:** Turn the wheels so the vehicle will not roll into the street, leave the vehicle in gear and set the parking brake.

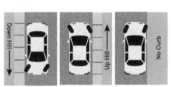

- **Headed downhill:** Turn your front wheels into the curb or right toward the side of the road.

Downhill: turn the wheels toward the curb.
Uphill: turn the wheels away from the curb.
No Curb: turn the wheels toward the shoulder of the road.

- **Headed uphill:** Turn your front wheels away from the curb (left) and let your vehicle roll back a few inches. The wheel should gently touch the curb.

- **Headed either uphill or downhill when there is no curb:** Turn the wheels so the vehicle will roll away from the center of the road if the brakes fail.

Parking at Colored Curbs

Painted colored curbs have special parking rules.

- **White:** Stop only long enough to pick up or drop off passengers.

- **Green:** Park for a limited time. The time limit may be posted on signs or painted on the curb.

- **Yellow:** Load and unload passengers and freight. Do not stop longer than the time posted. If you drive a noncommercial vehicle, you are usually required to stay with your vehicle.

- **Red:** No stopping, standing, or parking.

- **Blue:** Parking for a disabled person or someone driving a disabled person with a special placard or special license plate.

  — To learn more about disabled parking placards and license plates, visit **dmv.ca.gov/disabled-person-parking**.

Illegal Parking

Never park or leave your vehicle:

Example of crosshatched (diagonal lines) area.

- Where a No Parking sign is posted.
- On a marked or unmarked crosswalk.
- On a sidewalk, partially blocking a sidewalk, or in front of a driveway.
- Within three feet of a sidewalk ramp for disabled persons.
- In front of or on a curb that provides wheelchair access to a sidewalk.
- In the crosshatched (diagonal lines) area next to a designated disabled parking space.
- In a space designated for parking or fueling zero-emission vehicles, unless you are driving a zero-emission vehicle.
- In a tunnel or on a bridge, unless permitted by signs.
- Within 15 feet of a fire hydrant or fire station driveway.
- Between a safety zone and curb.

- Double parked.
- On the wrong side of the street or on a freeway, except:
  - In an emergency.
  - When a law enforcement officer requires a stop.
  - Where a stop is specifically permitted.

If you must stop on a freeway, park completely off the pavement and stay in your vehicle with the doors locked until help arrives. A vehicle that is stopped, parked, or left standing on a freeway for more than four hours may be removed.

Electric Vehicles

Local authorities can reserve parking spaces on public streets for electric vehicle charging.

DRIVING GREEN

Maximize your fuel efficiency while helping to lower emissions by following these practices:

- Speed up and slow down smoothly. Drive at a steady speed.
- Regularly inflate your tires, get oil changes, and check filters.
- Get rid of extra weight in your vehicle.

For more information, visit **fueleconomy.gov**.

LAW ENFORCEMENT STOPS

During a Law Enforcement Stop

- Turn on your right turn signal to acknowledge that you see the officer.
- Move completely onto the right shoulder, even if in the carpool/HOV lane. Stop in a well-lit area when possible.
- Turn off your radio.
- Remain inside your vehicle unless directed to get out by the officer.
- Roll down your window after stopping your vehicle and before the officer makes contact with you.
- The driver and all passengers should place their hands in clear view before the officer makes contact with them.

Beginning January 1, 2024, law enforcement officers must state the reason for a traffic or pedestrian stop before they begin questioning related to a criminal investigation or traffic violation. An exception is made if an officer reasonably believes withholding the reason is necessary to protect life or property from imminent threat. The reason for the stop must be documented on the citation issued or law enforcement report completed.

Your Rights During the Enforcement Stop

If an officer asks your permission to do something, you have a right to say no. However, if you say no and the officer says they are going to do it anyway, you do not have a right to interfere with their actions. For example, an officer may request to search part or all of your vehicle. You have a right to decline that request, but the officer may have the legal authority to search your vehicle anyway under certain circumstances. If you do not want the officer to search your vehicle, you should clearly say that you do not give your permission, but you do not have a right to resist or obstruct the officer if they search your vehicle anyway.

The driver of a stopped vehicle must produce a driver's license, proof of insurance, and vehicle registration when stopped by law enforcement. If a driver does not produce these documents, officers may conduct a limited search for them. An officer may also request the names or identification of passengers. Passengers can decline that request, but under some circumstances the passengers may be required to identify themselves anyway. If passengers do not want to produce their identification, they should clearly say so. Passengers should not interfere with the officer's duties in conducting the traffic stop, and if an officer demands identification, passengers should not interfere with the officer's actions. During a traffic stop, an officer can legally require the driver and all passengers to exit or stay inside the vehicle. If you are told to exit the vehicle or stay inside, you must do so.

In California, only federal law enforcement officers can ask you about your immigration status. California law prohibits state and local officers from asking drivers or passengers about their immigration status. If a California law enforcement officer asks you about your immigration status, you can decline to answer.

In general, the First Amendment protects the right of drivers and passengers to record interactions with law enforcement in public spaces. If you are recording, you should immediately make that clear. You do not have a right to interfere with the officer's lawful duties during the enforcement stop, and you should not reach into concealed areas to retrieve your recording device without the officer's permission. If your recording is not interfering with the officer's ability to lawfully do their job, an officer cannot confiscate your recording device, delete the recording, or destroy the device just because you are using it to record. In general, you also have the right to deny a request to unlock a cellular phone or provide a password to it, though under some circumstances, such as if you are on parole, you may have to give permission in response to such requests. Finally, no government employee can retaliate against you just because you recorded something in public.

Even if you believe your rights were violated, you should not engage in physical resistance or violence against the officer. If an officer does something that you believe violates your rights, you can voice your objection, but you should not physically resist. Everyone has the right to be safe during a traffic stop. Your safety and the officer's safety could be jeopardized if the situation escalates with physical resistance or violence.

All members of the public have a right to file a complaint against any law enforcement agency, and it is against the law for any government employee to retaliate against you for doing so. You can file a complaint with the law enforcement agency that employs the officer. You have a right to be free from discrimination based on your actual or perceived race, sex, color, ethnicity, national origin, age, religion, gender identity or expression, sexual orientation, mental or physical disability, medical condition, or citizenship status. You also have other rights guaranteed by the United States and California Constitutions, as well as California and federal laws. When you file a complaint, the agency that employs the officer must investigate the complaint. Links to contact information for California law enforcement agencies can be found at **post.ca.gov/le-agencies.**

I Am Not
A Mind Reader

Use your **Turn Signals**

Let others know **your intention** to change lanes or turn

SECTION 7. *Laws and Rules of the Road*

TRAFFIC CONTROL

When at or approaching traffic signals or signs, yield to pedestrians, bicyclists, and other nearby vehicles that may have the right-of-way. See Right of Way Rules: Who Goes First, in this section.

Traffic Signals

Solid Red Light

A red traffic signal light means STOP. You can turn right at a red light, if:

- There is not a NO TURN ON RED sign posted.
- You stop at the stop or limit line, yield for pedestrians, and turn when it is safe.

Red Arrow

A red arrow means STOP. Do not turn at a red arrow. Remain stopped until a green traffic signal light or green arrow appears.

Flashing Red Light

A flashing red signal light means STOP. After stopping, you may go when it is safe.

Solid Yellow Light

A yellow traffic signal light means CAUTION. The light is about to turn red. When you see a yellow traffic signal light, stop, if you can do so safely. If you cannot stop safely, cautiously cross the intersection.

Yellow Arrow

A yellow arrow means the protected turning time is ending. The signal will change soon. If you cannot stop safely or you are already in the intersection, cautiously complete your turn. Pay attention to the next signal. It could be a:

- Green or red traffic signal light.
- Red arrow.

Flashing Yellow Light

A flashing yellow traffic signal light is a warning to PROCEED WITH CAUTION. Slow down and be alert. You do not need to stop.

Flashing Yellow Arrow

You can turn, but your turn is not protected from other traffic. Proceed to turn left after yielding to oncoming traffic and proceed with caution.

Solid Green Light

A green traffic signal light means GO. You should still stop for any vehicle, bicyclist, or pedestrian in the intersection. Only proceed if you have enough space without creating a danger to any oncoming vehicle, bicyclist, or pedestrian. Do not enter the intersection if you cannot get completely across before the traffic signal light turns red.

Green Arrow

A green arrow means GO in the direction the arrow is pointing. The green arrow allows you to make a protected turn. Oncoming vehicles are stopped by a red traffic signal light.

Traffic Light Not Working

When a traffic light is not working, stop as if the intersection is controlled by STOP signs in all directions. Then proceed cautiously when it is safe to do so.

Pedestrian Signals or Signs

WALK or Walking Person
You may cross the street.

DON'T WALK or Raised Hand
You may not cross the street.

Flashing DON'T WALK or Flashing Raised Hand
Do not start crossing the street. The traffic signal light is about to change. Drivers must yield to pedestrians, even if the DON'T WALK light is flashing.

Numbers
The numbers count down the seconds left for crossing the street.

Diagonal Crossing
These are crisscross and diagonal crosswalks that allow pedestrians to cross the intersection in any direction at the same time. Cross only when the WALK signal allows it.

Sounds
Sounds such as beeping, chirping, or verbal messages help blind or visually impaired pedestrians cross the street.

Pedestrian Push Button
This is used to activate the WALK or Walking Person signal.

No Pedestrian Signals
If there are no pedestrian signals, obey the vehicle traffic signals.

Signs
Obey all warning signs regardless of their shape or color.

STOP Sign
Make a full stop before entering the crosswalk or at the limit line. If there is no limit line or crosswalk, stop before entering the intersection. Check traffic in all directions before proceeding.

Red YIELD Sign
Slow down and be ready to stop to let any vehicle, bicyclist, or pedestrian pass before you proceed.

Red and White Regulatory Signs

No U-Turn

No Left Turn

No Right Turn

White Regulatory Signs

Highway Construction and Maintenance Signs

Guide Signs

Hazardous Loads Placards

Slow Moving Vehicle

Warning Signs

Slippery
When Wet

Merging
Traffic

Divided
Highway

Two Way
Traffic

Lane Ends

End Divided
Highway

Traffic Signal
Ahead

Pedestrian
Crossing

Added Lane

Crossroad

Stop Ahead

Yield Ahead

Directional
Arrow

Curve

T
Intersection

Winding Road

*For more information, visit
dot.ca.gov.*

Red and White Regulatory Sign

Follow the sign's instruction. For example, DO NOT ENTER means do not enter the road or ramp where the sign is posted.

WRONG WAY Sign

If you enter a roadway against traffic, DO NOT ENTER and WRONG WAY signs may be posted. When it is safe, back out or turn around. If you are driving at night, you will know you are going the wrong way if the road reflectors shine red in your headlights.

Red Circle with a Red Line Through It

The picture inside the circle shows what you **cannot** do and may be shown with words.

Yellow and Black Circular Sign or X-shaped Sign

You are approaching a railroad crossing. Look, listen, slow down, and prepare to stop. Let any trains pass before you proceed.

Many railroad crossings also have a blue and white sign to tell you what to do if there is an emergency on or near the tracks, or if your vehicle has stalled on the tracks.

5-sided Sign

You are near a school. Drive slowly and stop for children in the crosswalk.

Diamond-shaped Sign

Warns you of specific road conditions and dangers ahead.

White Rectangular Sign

Communicates many important rules you must obey.

Warning Signs

Warns of conditions related to pedestrians, bicyclists, schools, playgrounds, school buses, and school passenger loading zones.

For more information about signs, visit **dot.ca.gov/programs/safety-programs/sign-charts**.

RIGHT-OF-WAY RULES: WHO GOES FIRST?

Right-of-way rules help you understand who goes first when vehicles, pedestrians, and bicyclists meet on the road. The vehicle that arrives to the intersection first has the right-of-way. Other vehicles, bicyclists, and pedestrians must wait for the person who has the right-of-way. Never assume that other drivers will give you the right-of-way. Give up your right-of-way when it will help prevent collisions.

Intersections

An intersection is any place where one road meets another road. Controlled intersections have signs or traffic signal lights. Uncontrolled and blind intersections do not. Before entering an intersection, check for vehicles, bicyclists, and pedestrians. Be prepared to slow down and stop if necessary. Pedestrians always have the right-of-way. Here are some right-of-way rules at intersections:

- **Without STOP or YIELD signs:** The vehicle that arrives to the intersection first has the right-of-way. However, if a vehicle, pedestrian, or bicyclist gets to the intersection at the same time as you, give the right-of-way to the vehicle, pedestrian, or bicyclist on your right. If you approach a stop sign and there is a stop sign on all four corners, stop first and proceed as above.

- **T intersections without STOP or YIELD signs:** Vehicles, bicyclists, and pedestrians on the through road (continuing to go straight) have the right-of-way.

- **Turning left:** Check for pedestrians. Give the right-of-way to any pedestrian or approaching vehicle that is close enough to be dangerous.

- **Turning right:** Always check for pedestrians crossing the street, and motorcycles and bicycles riding next to you.

- **Green traffic signal light:** Proceed with caution. Pedestrians have the right-of-way.

- **Entering traffic:** When entering traffic, you must proceed with caution and yield to the traffic already occupying the lanes. It is against the law to stop or block an intersection where there is not enough space to completely cross before the traffic signal light turns red.

Roundabouts

In a roundabout, traffic travels in one direction around a central island.

How to use a roundabout:

1. Slow down as you approach.
2. Yield to all traffic already in the roundabout.
3. Enter heading to the right when there is a big enough gap in traffic to merge safely.
4. Watch for signs and lane markings that guide you.
5. Travel in a counter-clockwise direction. Do not stop or pass.
6. Signal when you change lanes or exit.
7. If you miss your exit, continue around until you return to your exit.

If the roundabout has multiple lanes, choose your entry or exit lane based on your destination. This is shown in the image below. To:

1. Turn right (yellow car): Choose the right lane and exit in the right lane.
2. Go straight (red car): Choose either lane. Exit in the lane you entered.
3. Turn left: Enter and continue driving until you reach the exit in the direction you choose (blue car).

Roundabout Examples

Right Turn   Straight   Left Turn

Pedestrians

These are considered pedestrians or vulnerable road users:

- A person walking.
- A person traveling on something other than a vehicle or bicycle. This includes roller skates, a skateboard, etc.
- A person with a ***disability*** using a tricycle, quadricycle, or wheelchair for transportation.

| Tricycle | Quadricycle | Standard Wheelchair | Electric Wheelchair |

Although pedestrians have the right-of-way, they also must follow the rules of the road.

When there is a pedestrian crossing a roadway with or without a crosswalk, you **must** use caution, reduce your speed, or stop to allow the pedestrian to safely finish crossing.

Other things to keep in mind:

- Do not pass a vehicle stopped at a crosswalk. You may not be able to see a pedestrian crossing the street.
- If a pedestrian makes eye contact with you, they are ready to cross the street. Yield to the pedestrian.
- Always allow pedestrians enough time to safely cross a street as some groups such as seniors, people with small children, and people with disabilities may require extra time.

Crosswalks

A crosswalk is the part of the road set aside for pedestrians to safely cross the road. They are often marked with white lines. School crossings may have yellow crosswalk lines. Not all crosswalks are marked.

Pedestrians have the right-of-way in marked or unmarked crosswalks. If there is a limit line before the crosswalk, stop at the limit line and allow pedestrians to cross the street.

Some crosswalks have flashing lights. Whether or not the lights are flashing, look for pedestrians and be prepared to stop.

Pedestrians who are Blind

Pedestrians using guide dogs or white canes have the right-of-way at all times. These pedestrians are partially or totally blind. Be careful when you are turning or backing up. This is particularly important if you are driving a hybrid or electric vehicle because blind pedestrians rely on sound to know there is a vehicle nearby.

- Do not stop in the middle of a crosswalk. This could force a blind pedestrian to walk into traffic outside of the crosswalk.
- Do not honk your horn at a blind person.
- When a blind person pulls in their cane and steps away from the intersection, this gesture usually means you may go.

Mountain Roads

If two vehicles meet on a steep narrow road and neither vehicle can pass, the vehicle facing uphill has the right-of-way. The vehicle facing downhill has more control when backing up the hill. The vehicle facing downhill should back up until the vehicle going uphill can pass.

SHARING THE ROAD

Drivers need to share the road with other vehicles, pedestrians, bicyclists, road workers, and large vehicles.

Blind Spots (the No Zone)

Large vehicle and truck drivers have a better view in front of them and bigger mirrors. But they also have large blind spots, also called No Zones. In these areas, your vehicle can disappear from a large vehicle or truck driver's view. If you cannot see the truck's side mirrors, the truck driver cannot see you.

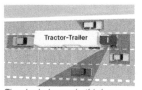

The shaded areas in this image are the truck driver's blind spots.

Braking

Large vehicles and commercial trucks take longer to stop than passenger vehicles traveling at the same speed. When traveling, they create extra space in front of their vehicle to use if they need to stop suddenly. The average passenger vehicle traveling at 55 mph can stop within 300 feet. A large vehicle traveling at the same speed can take up to 400 feet to stop. The heavier the vehicle and the faster it is moving, the longer it takes to safely stop, so a loaded truck will take longer to stop than an empty truck. Do not move in front of a large vehicle and suddenly slow down or stop. The large vehicle will not be able to stop fast enough to avoid crashing into you.

Turning
When a vehicle turns, the rear wheels follow a shorter path than the front wheels. The longer the vehicle, the greater the difference in the length of the turning path. This is why large vehicles and truck drivers must often swing wide to complete a turn. When you follow a large vehicle, look at its turn signals before you start to pass. It may appear to be turning one direction but instead is swinging wide in the opposite direction in order to turn.

Maneuvering
Large vehicles and trucks are not as easy to maneuver as passenger vehicles. On a divided highway with four or more traffic lanes in one direction, they may be driven in the lane just to the left of the far-right lane. When driving near large vehicles and trucks, do not:

- Change lanes directly in front of them to reach an exit or turn.
- Drive next to them longer than you need to. Always pass a large vehicle on the left side. After you pass the large vehicle or truck, move ahead of it. Driving alongside a large vehicle makes it hard for the driver to avoid dangers in the road.
- Underestimate their size and speed.

Buses, Streetcars, Trolleys
Safety zones are spaces set aside for pedestrians waiting for buses, streetcars, and trolleys. Safety zones are marked by raised buttons or markers on a road. Do not drive through a safety zone under any condition.

When a bus, streetcar, or trolley is stopped at a safety zone or traffic light, you may pass at no more than 10 mph.

Safety Zones are marked by dotted white lines.

Do not overtake and pass a light rail vehicle or streetcar on the left side, whether it is moving or standing, unless:

- You are on a one-way street.
- A traffic officer directs you to pass on the left.

Light Rail Vehicles

On public roads, light rail vehicles have the same rights and responsibilities as other vehicles. To safely share the road with light rail vehicles:

- Be aware of where they operate. Buildings, trees, and other items can cause blind spots for the operator.
- Never turn in front of an approaching light rail vehicle.
- Maintain a safe distance.

Do not turn in front of light rail vehicles.

- Check for approaching light rail vehicles before you turn across the tracks. Complete your turn only when the traffic light indicates you may proceed. Be aware they can interrupt traffic lights.

Motorcycles

Motorcyclists have the same rights and responsibilities as other vehicles. To safely share the road with motorcyclists:

- Check for motorcycles and use your mirrors when you change lanes or enter a road. Motorcycles are smaller in size and harder to see so they easily disappear in vehicle blind spots.
- Allow a safe three-second following distance. This space will help you avoid hitting a motorcyclist if they brake suddenly or fall.
- Whenever possible, give a motorcycle the full lane. It is legal to share lanes with motorcycles, this is known as lane splitting.
- Never try to pass a motorcycle in the same lane as you.
- Check for motorcyclists before you open your door next to traffic.
- When possible, move to one side of your lane to give motorcyclists more room to pass.

Road conditions can cause motorcyclists to suddenly change speed or direction.

Emergency Vehicles

Give the right-of-way to any law enforcement vehicle, fire engine, ambulance, or other emergency vehicle using a siren and red lights. Failure to pull over may result in a ticket. Drive to the right edge of the road and stop until the emergency vehicle(s) have passed.

Yield to emergency vehicles.

When approaching a stationary emergency vehicle with flashing emergency signal lights (hazard lights), move over and slow down.

If you are in an intersection when you see an emergency vehicle, continue through the intersection. Drive to the right as soon as it is safe and stop.

Obey any direction, order, or signal given by a law enforcement officer, or firefighter. Follow their orders even if they conflict with existing signs, signals, or laws.

It is against the law to follow within 300 feet of any fire engine, law enforcement vehicle, ambulance, or other emergency vehicle when their siren or flashing lights are on.

You can be arrested if you drive to the scene of a fire, collision, or other disaster. When you do this, you are getting in the way of firefighters, ambulance crews, or other rescue and emergency personnel.

Slow-moving Vehicles

They can take longer to get up to speed when entering traffic. Large trucks, bicycles, and some cars lose speed on long or steep hills. Some slow-moving vehicles have an orange and red triangle on their back, such as road maintenance vehicles, which usually travel at 25 mph or less.

An example of a slow-moving vehicle.

Other types of slow-moving motorized vehicles that may operate on public roads include:

- Scooters
- Neighborhood electric vehicles
- Golf carts

Adjust your speed to share the road with these vehicles.

Neighborhood Electric Vehicles (NEV) and Low-speed Vehicles (LSV)

Watch for slow-moving vehicles when you see these signs or markings:

- NEV USE ONLY
- NEV ROUTE

NEVs and LSVs reach a maximum speed of 25 mph. They are restricted from roads where the speed limit is greater than 35 mph.

Animal-drawn Vehicles

Horse-drawn vehicles and people riding horses or other animals are allowed to share the road with motor vehicles. It is against the law to intentionally scare horses or livestock.

Near Animals

If you see a sign with a picture of an animal, watch for animals on or near the road. If you see animals or livestock near the road, slow down or stop and proceed when it is safe. Be sure to follow directions from the person in charge of the animals.

Bicycles

Bicyclists have the same rights and responsibilities as other drivers. Bicyclists may:

- Legally ride on certain sections of freeways where there is no alternate route and bicycling is not forbidden by law.
- Move left to avoid hazards. These may include parked or moving vehicles, bicycles, animals, or trash.
- Choose to ride near the left curb or edge of a one-way street.
- Choose to use crosswalks by stopping and crossing as a pedestrian.

Bicyclist Responsibilities

As a bicyclist, you must:

- Obey all traffic signs, signal lights, and basic right-of-way rules.
- Ride in the same direction as traffic.
- Always look over your shoulder to make sure the lane is clear before turning or changing lanes.
- Yield to pedestrians.
- Wear a helmet (if under 18 years old).
- Stay visible (for example, never weave between parked vehicles).
- Ride as near to the right curb or edge of the roadway as possible.
- Not ride on the sidewalk (unless allowed by the city).
- Make left and right turns in the same way drivers do, using hand signals and turn lanes.
- Use a bike lane, whenever possible, or use a through traffic lane.
- Have fully functional brakes.

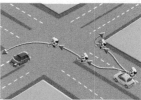

Examples of turns for bicyclists.

Intersections with special lanes for bicyclists.

Bicycling at Night

When it is dark out, bicyclists should avoid wearing dark clothing. Your bicycle must have the following equipment:

- A front lamp with a white light visible from 300 feet.
- A built-in rear red reflector, solid red light, or flashing red light. This must be visible from 500 feet.
- A white or yellow reflector on each pedal, the bicyclist's shoes, or their ankles. These must be visible from 200 feet.
- A white or yellow reflector on the front wheel, a white or red reflector on the rear wheel, or reflectorized tires.

Bicycling in Travel Lanes

Bicyclists traveling slower than the flow of traffic must ride as close as possible to the right curb or edge of the road, **unless**:

- Passing a vehicle or another bicycle in the same direction.
- Preparing to make a left turn.
- Avoiding a hazard or road condition.

- A lane is too narrow for a bicycle and a vehicle to safely travel side-by-side in the lane.
- Approaching a right turn.
- On a one-way road with two or more lanes. In this case, a bicyclist may ride near the left curb or edge of the road.

Drivers should follow at a safe distance. When it is safe, the bicyclist should move to a position that allows vehicles to pass.

Passing a Bicyclist

To safely pass a bicyclist that is in the travel lane, you may need to change to another lane. In this case, pass safely, then return to your original lane. Leave space between your vehicle and the bicyclist.

Right

Wrong

When you cannot change lanes to pass a bicyclist, allow at least three feet between your vehicle and the bicyclist. If you cannot give three feet of space, do not pass the cyclist until three feet of clearance can be given. This will help you avoid putting the bicyclist in danger. Remember to:

- Give bicyclists enough space so they are not forced into parked vehicles or open vehicle doors.
- Only merge toward the curb or into the bike lane when it is safe.
- Merge safely behind a bicyclist when preparing to make a turn.
- Enter a bike lane no more than 200 feet before starting a turn.
- Check for bicyclists when changing lanes or entering traffic. They may be hidden in a vehicle's blind spots.
- Be careful when approaching or passing a bicyclist on a two-lane road.

Road Workers and Work Zones

You will see warning signs and message boards when there are workers, slow-moving equipment, and closed lanes ahead.

Go through the work zone carefully by:

- Slowing down.
- Allowing extra space between vehicles.
- Expecting sudden slowing or stopping.
- Watching for drivers changing lanes.
- Avoiding distractions.

Cones, drums, or other barriers will guide you through the work zone. Prepare to slow down or stop for highway equipment. Merge as soon as it is safe without crossing the cones or drums. Watch for bicycles if lanes are narrow or the shoulder is closed. Obey special signs or instructions from workers such as flaggers.

Fines and Double Fine Zones

Fines for traffic violations in a work zone can be $1,000 or more. Anyone convicted of assaulting a highway worker faces fines of up to $2,000 and imprisonment for up to one year.

Certain roads are chosen as Safety Enhanced-Double Fine Zones. This is due to increased collision-related injuries and fatalities. Fines are doubled in these zones.

Fines are also doubled in highway construction or maintenance zones when workers are present.

Move Over and Slow Down

Drivers must move over and slow down for emergency and road work vehicles. These include:

- Stationary emergency vehicles or tow trucks displaying flashing amber warning lights.
- Stopped road work vehicles displaying emergency flashing or amber warning lights.

Vehicles with Hazardous Loads

A diamond-shaped sign on a truck means that the truck's load may be dangerous (gas, explosives, etc.). Vehicles with these signs **must** stop before crossing railroad tracks.

Examples of hazardous load placards.

Heavy Traffic or Bad Weather

You must drive slower when there is heavy traffic or bad weather. At the same time, you should not block normal and reasonable traffic flow by driving too slowly. Do not drive over or under the speed limit. You may be cited if you do. When another driver is close behind you and wishes to drive faster, move to the right. If you choose to drive slower than other traffic, drive in the right lane. Refer to Choosing a Lane in Section 6 for more information.

Towing

You must drive in the far-right lane or a lane marked for slower vehicles when you:

* Tow a vehicle or trailer.
* Drive a truck with three or more axles.

If no lanes are marked and there are four or more lanes in your direction, you may only drive in the two lanes closest to the right edge of the road.

Around Children

The speed limit is 25 mph within 500 feet of a school while children are outside or crossing the street. Some school zones may have speed limits as low as 15 mph. When near schools, look for:

All vehicles must stop for school buses.

* Bicyclists and pedestrians.
* School safety patrols or crossing guards. Be sure to obey their directions at all times.
* Stopped school buses and children crossing the street.
    — Some school buses flash yellow lights when preparing to stop to let children off the bus. The yellow flashing lights warn you to slow down and prepare to stop.

— When the bus flashes red lights (located at the top, front, and back of the bus), you must stop from either direction until the children are safely across the street and the lights stop flashing. Remain stopped while the red lights are flashing. If you fail to stop, you may be fined up to $1,000 and your driving privilege could be suspended for one year.
— If the school bus is on the other side of a divided or multilane highway (two or more lanes in each direction), you do not need to stop.

Blind Intersections

An intersection is considered blind if it has no stop signs at any corner.

If your view is blocked, move slowly forward until you can see. The speed limit for a blind intersection is 15 mph.

Alleys

An alley is any road no wider than 25 feet that is used to access the rear or side entrances of buildings or properties. The speed limit in an alley is 15 mph.

Near Railroad or Light Rail Tracks

The speed limit is 15 mph within 100 feet of a railroad crossing and you cannot see the tracks for 400 feet in both directions. You may drive faster than 15 mph if the crossing is controlled by gates, a warning signal, or a flagman. At railroad or train crossings:

- Flashing red warning lights indicate you must stop and wait. Do not proceed over the railroad tracks until the red lights stop flashing, even if the gate rises.
- When the crossing devices or a person warns you a train is coming, stop at least 15 feet from the nearest track.
- Do not go under lowering gates or around lowered gates. If the gates are lowered and you do not see a train approaching, call the posted railroad emergency toll-free number or 911.
- Stop, look, and listen. If you see a train coming or hear a horn or bell, do not cross. Many crossings have multiple tracks. Look in both directions and only cross when it is safe.

- Expect a train on any track, at any time, traveling in either direction.
- Never stop on the railroad tracks. Wait and do not begin proceeding if you do not have enough room to completely cross the tracks. If you are on the tracks, you risk injury or death.
- Watch for vehicles that must stop before they cross train tracks. These vehicles include buses, school buses, and vehicles marked with a hazardous materials placard.

Business or Residential Districts
The speed limit is 25 mph, unless otherwise posted.

OTHER IMPORTANT ROADWAY INFORMATION
You must:

- **Not** smoke when a minor is in the vehicle. You can be fined.
- **Not** dump or abandon animals on a highway. This crime is punishable by a fine of up to $1,000, six months in jail, or both.
- **Not** drive a vehicle so overloaded that you cannot control it, see ahead, or see to the sides of your vehicle.
- **Not** drive a vehicle with an unsecured load that is a safety hazard.
- **Not** carry anything in or on a passenger vehicle which extends beyond the fenders on the left side or more than 6-inches beyond the fenders on the right side.
  - Cargo that extends more than 4 feet from the back-rear bumper of the vehicle must display a 12-inch red or fluorescent orange square flag.
  - At night, this cargo must be marked with two red lights.
- **Not** allow a person to ride in the back of a pickup or other truck unless the vehicle has secure seats and seat (safety) belts.
- **Not** transport animals in the back of a pickup or other truck unless the animal is properly secured. This prevents the animal from falling, jumping, or being thrown from the vehicle.
- **Not** drive a vehicle equipped with a video monitor visible to the driver, unless it only displays vehicle information, navigation system, media player, or radio.
- **Not** throw a cigarette, cigar, or other flaming or glowing substance from your vehicle.

- **Not** put signs or other objects on the front windshield or side rear windows that block your view. Do not hang objects on the mirror. Objects may only be affixed in these locations:
  - A 7-inch square on the lower corner of the passenger's side windshield or the lower corner of the rear window.
  - A 5-inch square on the lower corner of the driver's side window.
  - On the side windows behind the driver.
  - A 5-inch square located in the center uppermost portion of your windshield for an electronic toll payment device.
- **Not** interfere with a funeral procession. A funeral procession is led by a traffic officer and has the right-of-way. All vehicles taking part in the procession have windshield markers to identify them and have their headlights on. You can be ticketed if you interrupt a funeral procession.
- **Not** operate a vehicle with an illegible license plate.
- **Not** alter a license plate in any way.

Evading Law Enforcement

It is a misdemeanor to use a motor vehicle to flee or attempt to evade law enforcement performing their duties. This is punishable by imprisonment in a county jail for one year or less.

A person convicted of causing serious bodily injury during a law enforcement pursuit is subject to imprisonment in a state prison for up to seven years, or a county jail for one year or less.

A person convicted of manslaughter resulting from evading law enforcement during a pursuit is subject to imprisonment in a state prison for a minimum of 4 to 10 years.

If an unlicensed person is caught driving your vehicle, it may be impounded for 30 days.

Speed Contests and Reckless Driving

A person convicted of reckless driving or engaging in a speed contest that causes injury to another person is subject to imprisonment, a fine, or both.

Points on Your Driver's Record

DMV monitors your driving record. If you are stopped by a law enforcement officer and cited (ticketed) for a traffic violation, you sign the ticket as a promise to appear in traffic court. If you get a traffic ticket and fail to appear (FTA) in court, DMV may suspend your driving privilege until you appear. If you do not keep your promise to appear in court, the FTA goes on your driver record.

Each time you are convicted of a moving traffic violation, the court notifies DMV. The conviction is placed on your driver's record. Convictions reported by other states and juvenile court are also added to your driver's record. Traffic convictions and collisions stay on your record for 36 months or longer, depending on the type of conviction. As an adult, your license may be suspended if your driver's record shows one of the following point totals:

- 4 points in 12 months.
- 6 points in 24 months.
- 8 points in 36 months.

Traffic Violator School

If you are given a one-point traffic violation, the judge may offer you the choice to attend a traffic violator school to have the citation not reported to your insurance company but remain on your driving record. You can do this once in any 18-month period. The school will report your course completion to the court. You will also get a completion receipt.

If you are a commercial driver cited in a noncommercial vehicle, see the *California Commercial Driver Handbook*.

Suspension or Revocation

If you have too many points on your driver's record, you will be considered a negligent driver. DMV will place you on probation, suspend, or revoke your driving privilege. When this happens, you have the right to a hearing. DMV will notify you in writing of any action taken against your driving privilege and inform you of your legal rights, including your right to a hearing.

DMV will revoke your driving privilege if you are convicted of a hit-and-run or reckless driving that resulted in injury. Courts also have the authority to suspend a person's driving privilege.

At the end of your suspension or revocation, you may apply for a replacement driver's license. You must show proof of financial responsibility (such as SR 22/SR 1P).

Maintaining Your Minor's (Provisional) Driver's License

If you get into collisions or commit traffic violations within the first 12 months of obtaining your minor's driver's license, DMV may restrict or suspend your driving privilege. You cannot drive if your driving privilege is suspended or revoked.

As a minor, DMV may take action against your license if you have:

- One at fault collision or traffic violation conviction: An at fault collision means you were found responsible.
- Two at fault collisions, two traffic violation convictions, or one of each: You cannot drive for 30 days unless a licensed adult, at least 25 years old, rides with you.
- Three at fault collisions, three traffic violation convictions, or a combination: Your driving privilege will be suspended for six months. You will be on probation for one year.
  - If you have more at fault collisions or traffic violation convictions while on probation, your license will be suspended again.
- A conviction of using alcohol or a controlled substance, or both and are 15-20 years old: The court will order DMV to suspend your driving privilege for one year or delay your eligibility to apply for a driver's license.

NOTE: Turning 18 years old does not erase or end existing restrictions, suspensions, or probation sentences.

Administrative Hearing

Administrative hearings are conducted by DMV. If you received notification that a proposed action is being taken against your driving privilege, you must request a hearing within 10 days of being served or 14 days from the date the notice is mailed. If you do not make a timely request, your right to a hearing will be lost.

This hearing provides you with an opportunity to be heard before an action is taken against your driving privilege. You may also have to appear in court for the same reason. Any action taken by the court is independent of the action taken by DMV.

Your Hearing Rights

You have the right to:

- Present relevant evidence and witnesses on your behalf.
- Testify on your behalf or be represented by an attorney or other representative at your expense. Representation by an attorney is not required.
- Review the evidence and cross examine the testimony of any witness. DMV bases its case only on written documents. If you wish to question someone who prepared a document or is listed on a document used as evidence, it is your responsibility to acquire a subpoena.

For more information regarding Administrative Hearings, visit **dmv.ca.gov/driversafety**.

Unsafe Driver

If you know someone who no longer drives safely, you may submit a Request for Driver Reexamination to DMV to review their driving qualifications. To obtain a form, visit **dmv.ca.gov/reexamination**.

RECORD CONFIDENTIALITY

Most information in your driver's record is available to the public, except physical or mental conditions, address, and social security number.

You can get a copy of your driver's record online or at a kiosk. For more information on record requests, visit **dmv.ca.gov/record-requests**.

SHARE the Road

Courtesy Counts

STATE OF CALIFORNIA

Department of Motor Vehicles

SECTION 8. *Safe Driving*

BE AWARE OF YOUR SURROUNDINGS

To drive safely, you need to know what is around you. This helps you make good decisions and react to hazards on the road. This image shows the areas around your vehicle.

- Green: Ahead of you.
- Blue: Next to you.
- Yellow: Blinds spots.
- Red: Behind you.

Scan Your Surroundings

To give yourself time to react, avoid last minute moves and hazards, always keep your eyes moving and scan the road at least 10 seconds ahead of your vehicle.

Tailgating (Following Too Closely)

Tailgating makes it harder for you to see the road ahead because the vehicle in front of you blocks your view. You will not have enough time to react if the driver in front of you brakes suddenly. Use the three-second rule to ensure a safe following distance and avoid a collision. Following other vehicles at a safe distance gives you enough time to react if another driver makes a mistake.

If a vehicle merges in front of you too closely, take your foot off the accelerator. This creates space between you and the vehicle ahead.

Create more space in front of your vehicle when:

- A tailgater is behind you. Maintain your course and speed. Then, when safe to do so, merge right to change into another lane and allow the tailgater to pass.
- Following motorcyclists on metal surfaces (bridge gratings, railroad tracks, etc.), and gravel.

Know What is At Your Side

Be aware of what is on each side of you. To maintain enough space to maneuver safely and react to other drivers:

- Do not stay in another driver's blind spot.
- Avoid driving directly alongside other vehicles.
- Make space for vehicles entering freeways, even if you have the right-of-way. Be ready for rapid changes and watch for signals from other drivers.
- Keep space between your vehicle and parked vehicles.
- Look both ways, even at intersections where traffic has a red light or stop sign.

Blind Spots

Every vehicle has blind spots. These are areas around the vehicle that a driver cannot see when looking straight ahead or using the mirrors. For most vehicles, the blinds spots are at the sides, slightly behind the driver.

The shaded areas are your blind spots.

To check your blind spots, look over your right and left shoulders out of your side windows. Only turn your head when you look. Do not turn your whole body or steering wheel. Check your blind spots before you:

- Change lanes.
- Turn at an intersection.
- Merge with traffic.
- Back up.
- Leave a parking space.
- Parallel park.
- Pull out from the curb.
- Open your car door.

Know What is Behind You

Knowing what is behind you can help you avoid rear-end collisions. Check traffic behind you often by using your rearview mirror, side mirrors, and turning your head:

- Change lanes.
- Check your blind spots.
- Reduce your speed.
- Turn into a side road or driveway.
- Stop to pull into a parking space.
- Pull up to and away from the curb.
- Back up.

UNDERSTAND THE ROAD CONDITIONS

Darkness

When driving at night, make sure you can stop in the distance lit by your headlights. Use your high-beam headlights when possible. This includes an open country or dark city streets. Do not use high-beam headlights in areas where they are illegal. Dim your high-beam headlights to avoid blinding the driver of an oncoming vehicle. If another vehicle's lights are too bright:

- Do not look directly into the oncoming headlights.
- Look toward the right edge of your lane.
- Watch the oncoming vehicle out of the corner of your eye.
- Do not react to the other driver by keeping your high-beam headlights on. This only makes it harder for both of you to see.

When it is dark outside or raining, use your low-beam headlights. Do not drive using only your parking lights. When you drive at night, remember:

- Motorcycles, pedestrians, and bicyclists are much harder to see.
- Highway construction can take place at night. Reduce your speed in highway construction zones.
- When you leave a brightly lit place, drive slowly until your eyes adjust to the darkness.
- When a vehicle with one light drives toward you, drive as far to the right as possible. It could be a bicyclist, motorcyclist, or vehicle with a missing headlight.

Sun Glare

To help manage sun glare:

- Keep the inside and outside of your windshield clean.
- Wear polarized sunglasses.
- Maintain enough space between your vehicle and the vehicles around you.
- Make sure your car visor works and is free of anything that would restrict use.
- Be aware of pedestrians. You may have difficulty seeing them.
- Try to avoid driving during sunrise and sunset.

Skids

A skid is when one or more of the tires lose traction with the road and the vehicle starts to slip. You may not be able to control your vehicle. There are a few different types of skids.

Slippery Surface Skids

Ice and packed snow on the road can cause your vehicle to skid. This is even more likely if you are driving too fast or going downhill. Drive slowly and leave space between your vehicle and the vehicle ahead of you. To prevent skidding on slippery surfaces:

- Slow down as you approach intersections and curves. For sharp curves, slow down as you approach and move through.
- Avoid fast turns and quick stops.
- Shift to low gear before going down a steep hill.
- Avoid areas like ice patches, wet leaves, oil, or standing water.

If you start to skid, follow these steps:

1. Slowly remove your foot from the accelerator.
2. Do not use the brakes.
3. Turn the steering wheel in the direction of the skid.
4. Try to get a wheel on dry pavement.

Locked Wheel Skids

A locked wheel skid is usually caused by braking too hard when you are going too fast. If this happens, your vehicle will skid no matter which way the steering wheel is turned. To get out of a locked wheel skid if your vehicle is equipped with:

- Four-wheel antilock braking system (ABS), apply firm pressure on the brake pedal.
- Rear-wheel ABS (common in light trucks):

- Ease up on the brake pedal while maintaining just enough pressure to allow the front wheels to roll again so you can steer.
- Stop braking and turn the steering wheel into the direction of the skid.

- Front-wheel ABS, remove your foot from the brake pedal to unlock the wheels. Steer in the direction you want to go and straighten the front wheels as the vehicle begins to straighten out.

NOTE: To determine if your vehicle has ABS, refer to the vehicle owner's manual.

If your vehicle is not equipped with ABS and begins to skid, quickly pump your brakes until you are at a safe speed. If you:

- Press the brake pedal and it sinks to the floor, quickly pump the brakes by gently applying and releasing pressure on your brake pedal.
- Pump the brakes, down shift your vehicle into a lower or neutral gear to slow down. Then try using your emergency brake to stop.

If your brakes get wet, you can dry them by lightly pressing the accelerator and brake pedals at the same time. Only do this until the brakes dry.

Slippery Roads

Rain, snow, or mud can make the roads slippery. Drive more slowly than you would on a dry road. Adjust your speed for different conditions:

- **Wet road:** Reduce your speed by 5 to 10 mph.
- **Packed snow:** Reduce your speed by half.
- **Ice:** Reduce your speed to no more than 5 mph.

Some road surfaces are more slippery than others when wet. These usually have warning signs posted. Here are situations where the road may be more slippery:

- Shade from trees or buildings can hide icy spots on cold, wet days. These areas freeze first and dry out last.
- Bridges and overpasses tend to freeze before the rest of the road. They can have icy spots.
- When it starts to rain, the pavement can be very slippery.

Slow down at the first sign of rain, drizzle, or snow on the road. This is especially true if it has been dry for some time because oil and dust on the road's surface have not been washed away.

Turn on your windshield wipers, low-beam headlights, and defroster. In a heavy rainstorm or snowstorm, you may not be able to see more than 100 feet in front of your vehicle. If you cannot see farther than 100 feet, it is not safe to drive faster than 30 mph. You may have to stop from time to time to wipe mud or snow off your windshield, headlights, and taillights. If you drive in snowy areas, carry snow chains for your tires. Snow chains give your tires more traction. Carry the correct number and type of chains for your vehicle.

Hydroplaning

Hydroplaning occurs when driving in wet or rainy conditions. Hydroplaning is a vehicle riding on water because the tires lose all contact with the road. A slight change of direction, applying the brakes, or a gust of wind could throw the vehicle into a skid. To avoid hydroplaning:

- Drive slowly.
- Steer around standing water, if possible.
- Slow down if you hear sloshing sounds from the tires.
- Slow down when changing lanes or direction.

If your vehicle starts to hydroplane:

- Slow down gradually.
- Do not use the brakes. Sudden braking may cause you to lose control of your vehicle.

Stuck in Snow or Mud

If stuck in the snow or mud, follow these steps:

1. Shift into a low gear and keep the front wheels straight.
2. Gently step on the accelerator. Avoid spinning the wheels.
3. Drive slowly forward as far as possible.
4. Shift into reverse and slowly back up as far as possible. Do not spin the wheels.
5. Shift into a low gear again and drive forward.
6. Repeat a forward-backward motion until the vehicle rolls free.
7. In deep mud or snow, put boards, tree branches, etc., under the tires. Only take this action when the vehicle is stopped.

Flooded Roads

Excessive water on a road may cause flooding. This can happen gradually or suddenly. It is important to understand the dangers of water on the road, including:

- Being swept off the road.
- Floating debris and unseen hazards.
- The road collapsing.
- Vehicle malfunction.
- Electrocution if there are fallen power lines.

It may not be possible to determine the depth of the flood by looking. If the water is deep, the road may be too dangerous to cross. It is best to find another route. If you have no other option but to drive through a flooded road, drive slowly. After you make it through the water, test your brakes to make sure they work correctly.

High Winds

High winds can be a hazard while driving. This is especially true for larger vehicles such as trucks, campers, and vehicles with trailers. When driving in high winds:

- Reduce your speed. This gives you better control over your vehicle. You will have more time to react if your vehicle gets hit by a strong gust of wind.
- Maintain a firm hand position on the steering wheel. Strong wind gusts are unpredictable. If you are not holding the wheel properly and a gust hits, you can lose control of the vehicle.
- Be alert. Look ahead and watch for any debris on the road. Give yourself enough time to react to road hazards.
- Do not use cruise control. Maintain maximum control of the accelerator if a gust occurs.
- Be proactive. It may be safer to pull over and wait for the storm to pass.

Fog or Heavy Smoke

It is best to avoid driving in heavy fog or smoke. Consider postponing your trip until the fog clears. If you must drive in heavy fog or smoke:

- Drive slowly.
- Use your low-beam headlights. High-beam headlights will reflect back and cause glare.
- Never drive using only your parking or fog lights.
- Make sure you can stop within the space you can see ahead.
- Increase your following distance.
- Use your windshield wipers and defroster as necessary.
- Avoid crossing lanes or passing traffic unless absolutely necessary.
- Listen for traffic you cannot see.

If the fog becomes too thick to drive safely, consider pulling off the road. Activate your emergency flashers and wait for conditions to improve.

Law Enforcement Traffic Breaks

During a traffic break, the officer turns on their emergency lights and slowly weaves across lanes. Law enforcement uses traffic breaks to:

- Slow or stop traffic to remove hazards from the road.
- Slow or stop traffic during heavy fog or unusual traffic conditions.
- Prevent collisions during unusual conditions.

You should:

- Turn on your emergency flashers to warn other drivers.
- Slowly decrease your speed to the same speed as the officer. Do not brake suddenly unless necessary to avoid a collision. Keep a safe distance from the patrol vehicle ahead of you.
- Not drive past the patrol vehicle. Do not speed up until the officer turns off their emergency lights and traffic conditions allow you to return to your normal speed.

PROTECT YOURSELF AND YOUR PASSENGERS

Seat Belts

You and your passengers must wear seat belts. You can get a ticket if you do not. If your passenger is under 16 years old, you can also get a ticket if they are not wearing their seat belt.

Wearing the lap belt and shoulder harness of a seat belt will increase your chance of survival in most types of collisions. This image shows what can happen in a collision.

IMPACT - If the red arrow were another car hitting your car on the driver's side:

1. You would first be thrown against the driver's side door,

2. Then you would "rebound" and be thrown toward the passenger's side door.

When you are in a collision, your vehicle stops. But you keep moving at the same speed you were traveling. You only stop when you hit the dashboard or windshield. If you are struck from the side, the impact could push you back and forth across the seat. Seat and shoulder belts keep you in a better position to control the vehicle. They may also minimize serious injuries.

It is important to wear the seat belt correctly to avoid injury or death:

- Wear the shoulder harness across your shoulder and chest. There should be little to no slack. Do not wear the shoulder belt under your arm or behind your back.
- Adjust the lap belt so that it is snug and lies low across your hips. Otherwise you might slide out of the belt in a crash.
- If you are pregnant, wear the lap belt as low as possible under your abdomen. Place the shoulder strap between your breasts and to the side of your abdomen's bulge.

Child Restraint System and Safety Seats

You must secure children with a federally-approved child passenger restraint system or safety belt. The requirements depend on the child's height and age.

- **Children who are under 2 years old, under 40 pounds, and under 3 feet 4 inches tall:** Secure in a rear-facing child passenger restraint system.

NOTE: A child in a rear-facing child passenger restraint system may not ride in the front seat of an airbag-equipped vehicle.

- **Children who are under 8 years old, or who are less than 4 feet 9 inches tall:** Secure in a child passenger restraint system in a rear seat. In some cases, children under 8 years old may ride in the front seat of a vehicle in a federally-approved child passenger restraint system. They may ride in the front seat if:
  - There is no rear seat.
  - The rear seats are side-facing jump seats.
  - The rear seats are rear-facing seats.
  - The child passenger restraint system cannot be installed properly in the rear seat.
  - All rear seats are already occupied by children 7 years old or younger.
  - Medical reasons prevent the child from riding in the back seat.

- **Children who are 8 years old or older, or at least 4 feet 9 inches tall:** May use a properly secured safety belt that meets federal standards.

Your local law enforcement agency or fire department can check the installation of your child passenger restraint system. As your child grows, check that the child passenger restraint system is the right size.

Air Bags

Air bags are a valuable safety feature on many vehicles. They can help keep you safer than a seat belt alone.

Ride at least 10 inches from the airbag cover, as long as you can maintain full control of your vehicle. Measure from the center of the steering wheel to your breastbone. Contact your vehicle dealer or manufacturer if you cannot safely sit 10 inches away from the air bag. They may have advice about additional ways to move back from your air bag. Passengers should also sit at least 10 inches away from the passenger-side air bag.

NOTE: Children seated next to a side air bag may be at risk of serious or fatal injury.

Unattended Children and Pets

It is illegal to leave a child who is six years old or younger unattended in a vehicle. A child may be left under the supervision of a person who is at least 12 years old.

It is dangerous and illegal to leave children or animals in a hot vehicle. The temperature inside a parked vehicle can rise rapidly when it is sitting in the sun. This is true even if a window is left slightly open. Too much exposure to heat can lead to dehydration, heat stroke, and death.

MANAGE YOUR SPEED

In California, you may never drive faster than is safe for the current road conditions. This is known as the Basic Speed Law.

Make sure you manage your speed and slow down when conditions call for it. Regardless of the posted speed limit, your speed should depend on:

- The number of vehicles on the road.
- The speed of other vehicles on the road.
- The road surface: smooth, rough, graveled, wet, dry, wide, or narrow.
- Bicyclists or pedestrians on or crossing the road.
- Weather: rain, fog, snow, wind, or dust.
- Traffic congestion: small changes in your driving habits can help reduce congestion. Avoid weaving in and out of freeway lanes.

There are also situations with specific speed limit laws and conditions where you should reduce your speed. Unless otherwise posted, the ideal maximum speed limit on most California highways is 65 mph. It is 55 mph on a two-lane undivided highway and for vehicles towing trailers.

CHOOSE BETWEEN HAZARDS

Sometimes dangers will be on both sides of the road at the same time. For example, parked cars to the right and oncoming cars to the left.

If one danger is greater than the other, give more space to the most dangerous situation. Suppose you are on a two-lane road with an oncoming vehicle to the left and a bicyclist ahead to your right. Instead of driving between the vehicle and the bicyclist, take one danger at a time. Slow down and let the oncoming vehicle pass. When the vehicle has passed, move to the left to allow plenty of space (at least three feet) to pass the bicyclist. If there is a steady flow of oncoming vehicles, use as much of the left lane as you safely can to pass the bicyclist.

KNOW HOW TO HANDLE EMERGENCIES

There are many types of emergencies you may encounter when you drive. Knowing how to handle emergencies can help keep you safe.

Tire Blowout and Accelerator Malfunction

If you have a tire blowout or accelerator malfunction:

1. Turn on your emergency flashers.
2. Hold the steering wheel tightly and steer straight ahead.
3. Slow down gradually by taking your foot off the accelerator slowly.

   — If your accelerator is stuck, shift to neutral and apply your brakes.
   — If you cannot shift to neutral, you should shut off the engine to initiate the vehicle slowing. DO NOT remove the key from the ignition.

4. Let the vehicle slow to a stop, completely off the road.
5. Fully apply the brakes when the vehicle is almost stopped.

Driving Off the Pavement

If your wheels drift off the pavement:

1. Grip the steering wheel firmly.
2. Remove your foot from the accelerator.
3. Brake gently.
4. Check for traffic behind you.
5. Carefully steer back onto the pavement.

Do not pull or turn your steering wheel with too much force. This may cause you to drive into oncoming traffic.

Overheating Conditions

In extreme heat, you should:

- Watch the temperature gauge.
- Avoid driving at high speeds for long periods.
- Turn off the air conditioner.

In extreme cold, you should:

- Watch the temperature gauge. The engine may not have the correct level of antifreeze.
- Use the defroster or slightly open your windows to keep them from fogging up.

NOTE: See the vehicle owner's manual for more information.

If Your Vehicle Becomes Disabled on the Freeway

If your vehicle stops working on the freeway:

1. Safely pull over to the right shoulder.
2. Exit on the right side so you are away from traffic if you must get out of the vehicle.
3. Dial 511 from your cell phone or locate call box for assistance..
4. Return to your vehicle as soon as you can. Get back into the vehicle from the right side (away from traffic).
5. Stay inside your vehicle with your seat belt on until help arrives.
6. Use your emergency flashers at your discretion. They can help other vehicles see you at night and in different weather conditions.

There are certain circumstances where it is safer to get out of your vehicle and stay away. These include situations where there is:

- Not enough space on the shoulder.
- A guardrail.
- An area for you to safely stay away from freeway lanes.

California Highway Patrol (CHP) Freeway Service Patrol (FSP)

During commute times, the CHP FSP provides free emergency roadside services in certain areas. If you get stuck on the freeway because your vehicle stops running, FSP will:

- Provide a gallon of gas if you run out.
- Jump start your vehicle if the battery is dead.
- Refill your radiator and tape hoses.
- Change a flat tire.
- Report a collision to CHP.

If FSP cannot start your vehicle, they will have it towed (free of charge) to a CHP-approved location. CHP will notify an auto club or towing service. FSP will not:

- Tow your vehicle to a private repair service or residence.
- Recommend tow service companies or repair and body shops.
- Tow motorcycles.
- Help vehicles which have been involved in a collision, unless they are directed to by CHP.

Call 511 for FSP information and assistance.

Disabled Vehicles on Railroad Tracks

If your vehicle stalls or stops while blocking part of a train track with a train approaching and warning lights flashing:

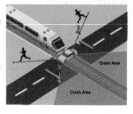

- Immediately exit your vehicle. Run away from the tracks diagonally in the direction the train is coming from. Then call 911.

If you do not see a train approaching and warning lights are not flashing:

- Exit your vehicle. Dial the number located on the railroad crossing posts or metal control box near the tracks. Provide the crossing number (if posted). Tell them a vehicle is on the tracks. Then call 911.

DO NOT DRIVE DISTRACTED

Avoid distractions while you drive. Some common distractions are:

- Looking at a phone, navigation system, children, and pets.
- Changing music or volume.
- Applying makeup or shaving.

CELL PHONES AND TEXTING

Cell phones are the main source of distracted driving. Driving while using a handheld cell phone is unsafe and illegal.

Adult drivers should only use a cell phone in hands-free mode when necessary.

- Do not answer your cell phone if it rings. Let the call go to voicemail.
- Do not send or read text messages or emails while driving.
- Mount your cell phone on the windshield, dashboard, or center console. It cannot block your view of the road.
- Use the single swipe or touch feature on the mounted cell phone.

MINORS AND CELL PHONES

It is against the law for a minor to use a cell phone or electronic wireless device to answer calls and send or respond to text messages while driving.

EXCEPTION: Minors may use a cell phone to make a call for emergency assistance.

BE FAMILIAR WITH NEW TECHNOLOGY

The technology in vehicles is always advancing. We will see more self-driving vehicles and vehicles with advanced driver assistance systems (ADAS) on the road. Vehicles with these systems may respond to road situations differently than a human driver would.

BE AWARE OF CARBON MONOXIDE

All gas-powered vehicles produce carbon monoxide. Carbon monoxide is a deadly odorless gas released from a vehicle's exhaust pipe. Never start your vehicle inside the garage with the door closed. Symptoms of carbon monoxide poisoning include:

- Tiredness
- Yawning
- Dizziness
- Nausea
- Headache
- Ringing in the ears

If you are experiencing any of these symptoms, have your exhaust system checked.

DISTRACTED DRIVING
Can Steer You into Danger

Keep both *hands on the wheel* and *eyes on the road*

STATE OF CALIFORNIA

Department of Motor Vehicles

SAFE *Driving Tips*

 Don't **drink and drive**

 Avoid **distractions**

 Buckle up

 Watch your **speed**

 Keep **both hands** on the **wheel**

STATE OF CALIFORNIA
DMV
Department of Motor Vehicles

SECTION 9. *Alcohol and Drugs*

California's driving under the influence (DUI) laws apply to both alcohol and drugs. It is illegal to drive while under the influence of alcohol or any drug that affects your ability to drive safely. As you age, your tolerance to alcohol decreases, which increases the risk of alcohol-related driving problems. The law does not see a difference between illegal drugs and medications you get from a doctor or pharmacy. They can all affect your ability to drive safely and react to what you see and hear.

No matter what age you are, it is illegal to drive after:

*   Drinking excessive amounts of alcohol in any form. This includes medications like cough syrup.
*   Taking any drug that affects your ability to drive. This includes prescriptions or over-the-counter medications.
*   Using any combination of alcohol or drugs that decreases your ability to drive safely.

Make sure you read medication labels and know the effects of any drug you use. If a law enforcement officer thinks you are driving while under the influence of drugs or alcohol, they have the right to ask you to take a blood or urine test. If you refuse to take one, DMV will suspend or revoke your driving privilege.

IMPORTANT: If you are 13 to 20 years old and convicted of operating a bicycle while under the influence of alcohol or drugs, your driving privilege may be suspended or delayed for one year once you are eligible to drive.

USE OR POSSESSION OF ALCOHOL OR CANNABIS PRODUCTS IN A VEHICLE

The law is very strict about carrying alcohol or cannabis products in your vehicle with you. It is illegal to drink any alcohol, to smoke or eat a cannabis product while you are driving or riding as a passenger in a vehicle. If you are carrying any alcohol, cannabis in your vehicle, the container must be sealed and unopened. If it is open, you must keep the container in the trunk or place where passengers do not sit. It is also illegal to keep an open container of alcohol in your glove box. This law does not apply if you are a passenger in a bus, taxi, camper, or motorhome.

BLOOD ALCOHOL CONCENTRATION (BAC) LIMITS

When you consume alcohol, traces of it enter your bloodstream. Your BAC measures how much alcohol is present in your bloodstream.

It is illegal for you to drive if you have a BAC of:

- 0.08% or higher if you are over 21 years old.
- 0.01% or higher if you are under 21 years old.
- 0.01% or higher at any age if you are on DUI probation.
- 0.04% or higher if you drive a vehicle that requires a commercial driver's license.
- 0.04% or higher if you are driving a passenger for hire.

If you drive with an illegal BAC, a law enforcement officer can charge you with DUI. Even if your BAC is below legal limits, that does not mean it is safe for you to drive. Almost everyone feels negative effects of alcohol, even at levels lower than the legal limit. Depending on how badly you are impaired, you may be arrested and convicted of a DUI even without a BAC measurement.

The table below shows BAC estimates based on how many drinks are consumed, gender, and body weight. Remember, even one drink can affect your ability to drive safely.

BLOOD ALCOHOL CONCENTRATION (BAC) Table for Male (M) / Female (F)									
Number of Drinks		Body Weight in Pounds							Driving Condition
		100	120	140	160	180	200	220	240	
0	M	.00	.00	.00	.00	.00	.00	.00	.00	Only Safe Driving Limit
	F	.00	.00	.00	.00	.00	.00	.00	.00	
1	M	.06	.05	.04	.04	.03	.03	.03	.02	Driving Skills Impaired
	F	.07	.06	.05	.04	.04	.03	.03	.03	
2	M	.12	.10	.09	.07	.07	.06	.05	.05	
	F	.13	.11	.09	.08	.07	.07	.06	.06	
3	M	.18	.15	.13	.11	.10	.09	.08	.07	
	F	.20	.17	.14	.12	.11	.10	.09	.08	
4	M	.24	.20	.17	.15	.13	.12	.11	.10	Legally Intoxicated
	F	.26	.22	.19	.17	.15	.13	.12	.11	
5	M	.30	.25	.21	.19	.17	.15	.14	.12	
	F	.33	.28	.24	.21	.18	.17	.15	.14	
Subtract 0.01% for each 40 minutes that lapse between drinks. 1 drink = 1.5 oz. 80 proof liquor, 12 oz. 5% beer, or 5 oz. 12% wine. Fewer than 5 persons out of 100 will exceed these values.										

NOTE: It is illegal to drink alcohol or take drugs when you are operating a boat, jet ski, water skis, aquaplane, or similar vessels. Learn more in the *California Harbors and Navigation Code.*

DUI ARRESTS

When you drive in California, you consent to a breath, blood, or urine test if a law enforcement officer suspects you of DUI. If you agreed to take a preliminary alcohol screening (PAS) or breath test, you may still be required to take a blood or urine test to detect the presence of drugs. If you refuse, DMV will suspend or revoke your driving privilege. If you are arrested for DUI:

- California's Administrative Per Se law requires DMV to suspend your driving privilege.
- The law enforcement officer may take your driver's license and give you a temporary driver's license for 30 days.
- You may request a DMV administrative hearing within 10 days from the date of your arrest.

DUI CONVICTIONS

If you are convicted of a DUI, DMV will suspend or revoke your driving privilege and you:

- Must complete a DUI program.
- Must file SR 22/SR 1P.
- Must pay any applicable license reissue or restriction fees.
- May be required to install an ignition interlock device (IID) on your vehicle.

Here are some additional penalties if you are convicted of DUI:

- You may be sentenced to up to six months in jail.
- You may have to pay a fine.
- Law enforcement may impound your vehicle and you may have to pay a storage fee.
- If you cause serious injury or death while driving under the influence of drugs or alcohol, you may face civil lawsuits.

All DUI convictions remain on your driver's record for 10 years. If you get any other DUIs during that time, the court or DMV may give you an additional penalty.

Drivers Under 21

If you are under 21 years old, there are additional laws for possessing and consuming alcohol.

Possessing alcohol:

- You may not carry any alcohol beverage inside a vehicle unless an individual who is 21 years old or older is with you. The container must be full, sealed, and unopened. If opened, the alcohol must be kept in the trunk or place where passengers do not sit.
  EXCEPTION: If you are working for someone with an off-site liquor sales license, you may carry alcoholic beverages in closed containers.
- If you are caught with alcohol in your vehicle, law enforcement can impound your vehicle for up to 30 days. The court may fine you and suspend your driver's license for one year. If you do not already have a driver's license, the court may ask DMV to delay giving you your first driver's license for up to one year.

Consuming alcohol:

- If a law enforcement officer suspects you of consuming alcohol, they can require you to take a hand-held breath test, PAS, or another chemical test.
- If you are convicted of a DUI with a BAC of 0.01% or higher, DMV may revoke your driving privilege for one year. You must also complete a licensed DUI program.
- If your PAS shows a BAC of 0.05% or higher, the officer may require you to take a breath or blood test.
- If a later test shows you have a BAC of 0.05% or higher, you may be arrested for a DUI and your driving privilege may be suspended.

Am I Okay TO DRIVE?

Buzzed Driving
is Drunk Driving

Designate a sober driver

SECTION 10. *Financial Responsibility, Insurance Requirements, and Collisions*

You must have your proof of financial responsibility (insurance) when you drive and for a drive test. If you get into a collision, you must show proof to the other drivers involved in the collision.

INSURANCE REQUIREMENTS

Your insurance must cover at least:

- $15,000 for a single death or injury.
- $30,000 for death or injury to more than one person.
- $5,000 for property damage.

Parents or guardians take on financial responsibility for drivers younger than 18 years old and pay for damages if the driver is involved in a collision. Drivers who are 18 years old and older take on their own financial responsibility.

Before you buy insurance, make sure that the agent, broker, or insurance provider is licensed by the California Department of Insurance. For more information, visit **insurance.ca.gov/license-status/**.

Low-cost Insurance

If you cannot afford liability insurance, you may be eligible for the California Low Cost Automobile Insurance Program. For more information, visit **mylowcostauto.com** or call 1-866-602-8861.

COLLISIONS

Understand factors that lead to collisions so you can try to avoid them.

Causes of Collisions

The most common causes of collisions are:

- Driver distractions.
- Unsafe speed.
- Improper turns.
- Not following the right-of-way rules.
- Not following stop signals and signs.
- Driving on the wrong side of the road.
- A vehicle traveling faster or slower than the flow of traffic.

If you see a vehicle's emergency flashers ahead, slow down. There may be a collision or other road emergency. Pass carefully.

Avoid driving near collisions, if possible. If anyone is injured, they will get help faster if other vehicles are not blocking the road.

What to Do if You Are in a Collision

If you are in a collision:

- You must stop. Someone could be injured and need your help. Failing to stop or leaving the scene of an accident is called a hit-and-run. The punishment is severe if you are convicted of a hit-and-run.
- Call 911 right away if anyone is hurt.
- Move your vehicle out of traffic if no one is hurt. Then call 911.
- Show your driver's license, vehicle registration card, insurance information, and current address to the other driver, law enforcement officer, and anyone else involved in the collision.
- You must make a report to law enforcement within 24 hours of the collision if anyone is injured or killed. Your insurance agent, broker, or legal representative can also file the report.
- Try to find the owner if your vehicle hits or rolls into a parked car or other property. If you cannot find the owner, leave a note with your name, phone number, and address. Securely attach the note to the vehicle or property. Report the collision to law enforcement.
- If you kill or injure an animal, call the nearest humane society or law enforcement. Do not try to move an injured animal.

Reporting a Collision

If you are in a collision, you must report it to DMV within 10 days if:

- The collision caused more than $1,000 in damage to property.
- Anyone was injured or killed. This applies even if the injuries were minor.

Each driver must file a Report of Traffic Accident Occurring in California (SR 1) with DMV at **dmv.ca.gov/accidentreport**. You (or your representative) must file a report whether or not you caused the collision. This applies even if the collision happened on private property.

Your driving privilege will be suspended if you fail to file a report. Law enforcement will not make a report for you.

Driving Without Insurance

Your driving privilege will be suspended for up to four years if you are in a collision and do not have proper insurance coverage. It does not matter who was at fault.

You can get your driver's license back during the last three years of the suspension if you provide a California Insurance Proof Certificate (SR 22/SR 1P) and maintain it during the three-year period.

COLLISIONS ON YOUR DRIVER'S RECORD

If you are involved in a collision resulting in $1,000 in damage, or where anyone is injured or dies, it is your responsibility to report the collision to DMV. DMV will add it to your driver's record. It does not matter who caused the collision.

SECTION 11. *Vehicle Registration Requirements*

You need to register your vehicle in California to use it in the state. For more information, visit **dmv.ca.gov/vrservices**.

BUYING OR SELLING A VEHICLE

When you buy a vehicle, you have 10 days to transfer ownership to your name.

When you sell a vehicle, you must notify DMV within five days by completing a Notice of Transfer and Release of Liability at **dmv.ca.gov/nrl**.

OUT-OF-STATE VEHICLES

You have 20 days to register your vehicle after you become a resident or get a job in California. For more information, visit **dmv.ca.gov/outofstatevr**.

All vehicles registered in California are required to meet California requirements including vehicle emission controls in support of California's clean air standards. DMV cannot register a vehicle if it does not qualify.

SAVE the Space
Need a Written Reminder?

Fraudulent use of a
Disabled Parking Placard
is *Against the Law*

SECTION 12. *Driver Safety*

Eventually, every driver will need to evaluate and assess their driving skills and abilities. If you are concerned about your driving, ask a trusted driver with a valid driver's license to sit in the passenger seat and observe your driving. Your observer should note any dangerous driving behaviors and give suggestions for improvement. Listen carefully and apply what you have learned. Consider professional driving lessons or driving classes as an alternative.

Reexamination

The *Vehicle Code* allows DMV to investigate and reexamine every driver's ability to operate a motor vehicle safely. A physical or mental condition or poor driver's record can be the basis for a reexamination, not a driver's age. Drivers with a physical or mental condition can be referred to DMV by a physician, law enforcement, or family member by submitting a completed Request for Driver Reexamination form.

Cognitive disorders, such as dementia, seizure disorder, brain tumor, Parkinson's disease, stroke, or vertigo, present a significant challenge to safe driving. Individuals suffering from these conditions may lose their ability to drive safely.

NOTE: When a referral or diagnosis for someone with a mild cognitive impairment is received by DMV, the Driver Safety team will schedule a reexamination. For more information regarding the reexamination process, visit **dmv.ca.gov/reexamination**.

DMV may do the following:

- Request medical information from you or your physician.
- Conduct an in-person or over the telephone reexamination.
- Require you to take a knowledge, vision, or driving test(s).
- Issue you a limited term driver's license.
- Immediately suspend or revoke your driving privilege if your physical or mental condition presents an immediate threat to public safety.
- Take no action against your driving privilege.

Priority Reexamination

If you come in contact with law enforcement and receive a Notice of Priority Reexamination of Driver with a check mark in the top box, carefully read the form. You have five working days to contact DMV to initiate the process or your driving privilege will be automatically suspended.

Driver's License Restrictions

DMV places restrictions on a driver's license to ensure a driver is operating a vehicle within their ability. Restrictions may be imposed by DMV or required by law. Restrictions placed on your driving privilege will be reasonable and necessary for your safety and the safety of others. Restrictions and conditions may include:

- Requiring a driver to place special mechanical devices on their vehicle, such as hand controls.
- Limiting when and where a person may drive, such as no night or freeway driving.
- Requiring eyeglasses or corrective contact lenses.
- Requiring additional devices, such as outside mirrors.

NOTE: There are no specific restrictions for seniors. All restrictions are based on conditions, not age.

Any restriction placed on your driver's license is based on the examiner's findings and recommendations.

What's the *RUSH?*
SPEED KILLS

Driving is a privilege - NOT a right
Obey posted speed limits

SECTION 13. *Seniors and Driving*

Senior drivers often have unique needs and concerns about driving. Driving requires certain physical, visual, and mental abilities. We all want to continue driving as long as we can. However, the time may come when we must limit or stop driving temporarily or permanently. Here are some warning signs of an unsafe driver:

- Getting lost in familiar places.
- Dents and scrapes on the car, fences, mailbox, garage doors, etc.
- Frequent close calls or collisions.

Senior drivers may consider:

- Limiting or not driving at night.
  - If night driving is necessary, choose a well-lit route.
- Driving during the time of day when traffic is light.
- Avoiding difficult intersections.
- Driving for short distances or limiting driving to essential places.
- No freeway driving.
- Installing an additional right-side mirror.

To get the Driver Skills Self-Assessment Questionnaire, visit **dmv.ca.gov/driver-skills**.

Driver's License Renewal

If you are 70 years old or older at the time your driver's license expires, you are required to renew your driver's license in person, unless otherwise instructed by DMV. Knowledge and vision tests are required. If you do not pass, you may be issued a temporary driver's license. DMV sends a renewal notice to your address of record about 60 days before your driver's license expires. If you do not receive a renewal notice, complete a Driver License or Identification Card Application at **dmv.ca.gov/dlservices** or at a DMV office. Visit **dmv.ca.gov/driver-ed** for more information and sample tests.

DMV's Senior Ombudsman

The Senior Ombudsman's primary function is to represent the interests of public safety for all Californians with a focus in addressing the concerns of senior drivers. Ombudsmen can assist as a go-between to ensure that senior drivers are treated fairly, consistent with laws and regulations, and with dignity and respect. While the Senior Ombudsman cannot represent you in a DMV hearing or reexamination, the Ombudsman can provide you with tools and information.

For information about driving as a senior, contact the Senior Ombudsman Program in your area:

Los Angeles and Central Coast Counties (310) 615-3552

Sacramento and Northern California Counties
(916) 657-6464 or (916) 657-7109

Orange and San Diego Counties (714) 705-1588

San Francisco, Oakland, and Bay Area (510) 563-8998

Cognitive Impairment

Seniors suffering from dementia present a significant challenge to safe driving. Individuals with progressive dementia ultimately lose their ability to drive safely. It is often up to caregivers, physicians, and law enforcement, to stop these seniors from driving and arrange alternative transportation. For more information about the reexamination process, visit **dmv.ca.gov/reexamination**.

Mature Driver Program

The Mature Driver Improvement Program is an eight-hour course for drivers 55 years old and older. It covers a range of topics that are of special interest to mature drivers.

Your insurance company may offer discounts if you complete the program. Contact your insurance provider with a copy of your completion certificate. Your certificate is valid for three years. You can renew it by completing another four-hour course.

You can take the course through DMV-approved providers. Visit **dmv.ca.gov/seniors** for more information, including locations near you.

Senior ID Cards

If you are 62 years old or older, you are eligible for a no-fee Senior ID card. Drivers of any age who are unable to continue driving safely due to a physical or mental condition may be eligible to exchange their driver's license for a no-fee ID card. The ID card serves as identification only. Details may be found at **dmv.ca.gov/id-cards**.

SECTION 14. *Glossary*

TERM	DEFINITION
Behind-the-wheel drive test	A drive test where you have control of the vehicle and are accompanied by a DMV examiner who is evaluating your driving skills.
Blood alcohol concentration (BAC)	Your BAC is the amount of alcohol in your blood. For example, if your BAC is 0.10%, that means you have 0.10 grams of alcohol in 100 milliliters of blood.
Driving performance evaluation (DPE)	DPE is the portion of the behind-the-wheel drive test when you drive your car with a DMV examiner who evaluates your driving skills.
Pedestrian	A pedestrian can also be a person with a disability using a tricycle, quadricycle, or wheelchair for transportation.
Right-of-way	Helps determine who is allowed to go first in situations where vehicles, pedestrians, and cyclists meet on the road.
Three-second rule	A driving rule that helps you estimate how closely you should follow other vehicles. When the vehicle in front of you passes a certain point, such as a sign, count three seconds. If you pass the same point before you finish counting, you are following too closely.
Traffic citation	Also known as a ticket, a traffic citation is an official summons issued by law enforcement for violating a traffic law.
Vulnerable road users (VRU)	VRUs are non-motorized road users, such as cyclists, pedestrians, and persons with disabilities or reduced mobility and orientation using a wheelchair, tricycle, or quadricycle.
Yield	Yield means to wait for, slow down, and be ready to stop (if necessary) to allow other vehicles or pedestrians who have right-of-way to proceed.

We know your time is *valuable*

GOONLINE
dmv.ca.gov/online

- Renew driver's license and vehicle registration
- Replace sticker or registration
- Change address
- Request driver's record
- Order vehicle record
- And more

STATE OF CALIFORNIA

Department of Motor Vehicles

GO PAPERLESS!

Opt-in for paperless notices for your driver's license, ID card, or vehicle registration.

Make your selection at
dmv.ca.gov/paperless

GO ONLINE
dmv.ca.gov/online

 Reduce, reuse, recycle this handbook.

STATE OF CALIFORNIA
Department of Motor Vehicles

DL 600 ENGLISH (REV. 1/2023)